143 Questions & Answers About George Washington

143 QUESTIONS & ANSWERS
ABOUT GEORGE WASHINGTON

FRANK E. GRIZZARD, JR.

MARINER
PUBLISHING

Buena Vista, Virginia

Mariner Publishing

All rights reserved.
Manufactured and Printed in the United States of America

Copyright © 2009 by Frank E. Grizzard, Jr.

First Published 2009
1 3 5 7 9 8 6 4 2

**Library of Congress Cataloging-in-Publication Data
Control Number: 2008941031**

143 Questions & Answers About George Washington
Frank E. Grizzard, Jr.

p. cm.

Includes bibliographical references and index.
ISBN 978-0-9820172-5-8 (softcover : alk. paper)
1. Washington, George, 1732–1799
2. Presidents—United States—Biography.
I. Grizzard, Frank E., Jr. II. Title.

Mariner Publishing
a division of
Mariner Media, Inc.
131 W. 21st Street
Buena Vista, VA 24416
http://www.marinermedia.com

Some of the text of this book has been adapted from *George!
A Guide to All Things Washington*, copyright by the author, 2005.

The Compass Rose and Pen is a Trademark of Mariner Media, Inc.

For Harlan R. Crow

Contents

Preface

This little book started out as one hundred questions and answers about George Washington. My objective was to offer brief answers to many of the questions frequently asked about Washington, dispelling some myths and clearing up some confusion along the way. But Washington is not easily confined and before I knew it I had passed my target without meeting my purpose. Perhaps a thousand questions and answers would make more sense, but then it would cease to be a little book. Likewise, the answers to many of the questions do not lend themselves to brevity although I have attempted to keep them as succinct as possible.

Once again I owe a debt of gratitude to the staff of Mariner Publishing. In particular, I wish to thank my publisher, Andy Wolfe, for his multiple readings of the manuscript and his many valuable suggestions; Judy Rogers for carefully proofreading the manuscript; Beth Wilkins for the cover design; and Tracy Lee Staton for the internal book design. I would also like to thank Jim Rees of the Mount Vernon Ladies' Association and Ed Lengel of the Papers of George Washington for reading and commenting on the manuscript.

It is natural to view with keen attention the countenance of an illustrious man, with a secret hope of discovering in his features some peculiar traces of excellence, which distinguishes him from and elevates him above his fellow mortals. These expectations are realized in a peculiar manner in viewing the person of General Washington. His tall and noble stature and just proportions—his fine, cheerful, open countenance—simple and modest deportment—are all calculated to interest every beholder in his favor, and to command veneration and respect. He is feared even when silent, and beloved even while we are unconscious of the motive.

—James Thatcher, Journal entry, 1779

As a boy, he gave no promise of the greatness that he was one day to achieve. He was ignorant of the commonest accomplishments of youth. He could not even lie.
—Mark Twain, in *The Celebrated Jumping Frog of Calaveras County, and Other Sketches,* 1867

George and Mary Washington with Martha's grandchildren,
Eleanor Parke Custis and George Washington Parke Custis
(Library of Congress)

1   Was George Washington ever a child?

No. George Washington was born wearing a powdered wig and three-cornered hat, army uniform, and riding boots. His wooden teeth pulled down his frowning jaws—in fact, at his birth he looked much like the portrait that appears on the dollar bill, painted by Gilbert Stuart when Washington was eight years old. To Washington belongs the singular credit of being the Father of His Country when he was but an infant.

Seriously.

> *Washington is the last person you would ever suspect*
> *of having been a young man with all the bright hopes and*
> *black despairs to which young men are subject.*
>
> —Samuel Eliot Morison,
> *The Young Man Washington*, 1932

2   Who were George Washington's parents?

Mary Ball and Augustine Washington, Sr., who married on 6 March 1731. Eventually they had six children, of whom George was their first.

Augustine, born in 1694, was a middle-class planter in Westmoreland County, Virginia. He attended Appleby School in England for several years and in 1715 married his first wife, Jane Butler, an orphan of Westmoreland, who bore four children before dying in 1729. Active in the civic and political affairs of his neighborhood, Augustine was an enterprising entrepreneur who served as agent for the Principio Iron Works and felt comfortable buying, selling, and leasing lands in speculative deals. He eventually accumulated ten thousand acres of land and owned about fifty slaves.

Augustine Washington was described by one who knew him as a gentle man, "remarkable for the mildness, courtesy, and amiability of his manners." He was also handsome, and at six feet unusually strong—so powerful it was said, that he could "raise up and place in a wagon a mass of iron that two ordinary men could barely raise from the ground." Family tradition says that Augustine caught cold while riding in a storm and died of complications shortly afterward, in April 1743—a death similar to that of his famous son nearly fifty-seven years later. Augustine was buried in the family vault at Popes Creek, near George's birthplace.

George Washington's mother, Mary Ball Washington, was like her husband's first wife, an orphan. She was born in Lancaster County, Virginia, and called the Rose of Epping Forest, after her father's estate. Mary bore six children to Augustine Washington, George being the eldest, followed by Betty, Samuel, John Augustine, Charles, and Mildred. (All lived to adulthood except Mildred, who died as an infant.) When Augustine died Mary chose not to remarry. She raised her children alone and with assistance from farm managers ran Ferry Farm, George's boyhood home.

Mary Washington moved into Fredericksburg in 1772, into a modest white frame house on the corner of Charles and Lewis Streets. There she lived in relative comfort for the rest of her life. Even when she was eighty years old she preferred to live alone with a few servants rather than move in with her daughter, Betty Lewis, who lived nearby at Kenmore plantation. In 1789 Mary died of breast cancer and was interred at Kenmore. In 1894 a fifty-foot granite obelisk monument was erected not far from her grave, and in 1891 the Association for the Preservation of Virginia Antiquities acquired Mary's house in Fredericksburg. A state university named in her honor is also nearby.

3   Is anything known about George Washington's ancestry and family?

Yes, although Washington took little interest in his genealogy. The family of de Wessyngton can be traced back at least to the late twelfth century, living in northern England near the border of Lancashire and Westmoreland. About seventy-five years before his birth, Washington's great-grandfather John settled in Virginia, at Bridge's Creek on the Potomac River in Westmoreland County. John Washington's line of descent went back to a wool merchant named Lawrence Washington, born about 1500, who became mayor of the town of Northampton in 1532.

Of the many Washington family members who can be identified with some certainty, one of the most interesting is George's great-great-grandfather Lawrence who served first as a lecturer and proctor at Oxford and then as rector of All Saints, Purleigh Parish, Essex, where in 1643 he was removed on charges of being a "common frequenter of Ale-houses, not only himself sitting daily tippling there, but also encouraging others in that beastly vice." Lawrence's parishioners acknowledge that he was "oft drunk" but helped him secure a new position preaching at Little Braxted, Essex, where he remained until his death a decade later.

Less is known about Washington's maternal ancestry. Washington's great-great-grandfather, William Ball, had been an attorney for the office of pleas and exchequer, and his great-grandfather, also named William, had immigrated to Virginia in 1657, establishing himself as a planter and trader. William settled in Lancaster County, where he won enough prominence to get elected to the Virginia House of Burgesses and to be named major of the county militia.

4 Is it true that Washington and his mother did not like each other?

That probably is an overstatement, although their relationship often has been characterized as devoid of affection. The record is meager, but what does survive shows that Washington was a dutiful—if not demonstrably affectionate—son.

For instance, Washington gave his mother the use and income of his Ferry Farm plantation, which he inherited in 1743, until the 1770s when she decided to move into Fredericksburg. He then took on the burden of handling her financial affairs. Washington occasionally visited Mary in Fredericksburg, and he appeared sad following his visit on the eve of his leaving for his presidential inauguration in 1789, when he perceived that she probably would not live long enough to see his return from New York. Washington knew that his sister Betty Lewis, who lived a couple of blocks away from their mother, was looking out for Mary's welfare.

> *Awful and affecting as the death of a parent is, there is consolation in knowing that Heaven has spared ours to an age beyond which few attain, and favored her with the full enjoyment of her mental faculties and as much bodily strength as usually falls to the lot of fourscore. Under these considerations and a hope that she is translated to a happier place, it is the duty of her relatives to yield due submission to the decrees of the Creator. When I was last at Fredericksburg, I took a final leave of my Mother, never expecting to see her more.*
> —George Washington to Betty Lewis, 1789

On the other hand, Washington did not write his mother very often, and Mary apparently never visited Mount Vernon. In fact, after the Revolutionary War, when Mary indicated that she was interested in coming to Mount Vernon for an extended visit, George discouraged her, saying it would not "answer purposes in any shape whatsoever." (It is unknown whether Mary and Martha liked one another.) For Mary's part, she thought nothing of demanding George's attention for trivial matters, whether he was out on the Virginia frontier or commanding the Continental army against the British in Boston. Mary never appeared to be fazed by her son's achievements or fame.

> *Nor, indeed, could you be retired in any room in my house; for what with the sitting up of company, the noise and bustle of servants, and many other things, you would not be able to enjoy that calmness and serenity of mind, which in my opinion you ought now to prefer to every other consideration in life.*
> —George Washington to
> Mary Washington, 1787

5   When is George Washington's birthday?

Eleven and 22 February 1732. Yes, two birthdays! No wonder people are confused! It was so even during Washington's life. The reason for the confusion is that the old-style calendar entry of 11 February 1731/32 became obsolete in 1752, when the British corrected their calendar by adding eleven days. This made Washington's birth date under the new style 22 February 1732.

It seems confusing, but it is not really. New Year in the Julian calendar (which Britain followed until 1752) began on 25 March; in the Gregorian calendar (to which much of Europe converted in 1582) on 1 January. Thus any date from 1 January through 24 March was indicated by a slash, representing the two calendars. (The dates 25 March to 31 December were the same in both calendars.) The extra eleven days added to the Gregorian calendar compensated for the inaccuracies that had resulted after hundreds of years of computing dates by the Julian method, despite the use of leap years.

6   Well, when did Washington celebrate his birthday?

In the eighteenth century birthday celebrations were not as common as now, and in fact many people did not even know their actual birthday. Washington did not celebrate his birthday at all until the public began to do so, during the Revolutionary War. One of the earliest public celebrations took place at the Continental army encampment at Valley Forge, Pennsylvania, on 22 February 1778, when army musicians serenaded their commander in chief. By 1784 many in America were beginning to think of Washington's birthday celebrations as a fitting way to honor the victorious American general; although according to his own diary entries Washington continued to busy himself with his typical plantation routine on his birthdays.

By 1778 Washington was celebrating his birthday, although with some ambivalence, on both 11 and 22 February. As he described it, "In reply to your wish to know the Presidents birthday it will be sufficient to observe that it is on the 11th of February *Old Style*; but the almanack makers have generally set it down opposite to the 11th day of February of the present Style; how far that may go towards establishing it on that day I dont know; but I could never consider it any other ways than as stealing so many days from his valuable life as is the difference between the old and the new Style."

On a side note, Washington's birthday is still an official holiday for federal workers, although the Uniform Holiday Bill of 1968 guaranteed that the day always be observed on the third Monday in February—always too early or too late to celebrate either the 22d or the 11th! President Richard M. Nixon's executive proclamation declaring that federal workers celebrate Washington's birthday in 1971 led to the erroneous conclusion that Nixon was responsible for the change.

> *George Washington Son to Augustine & Mary his Wife was born the 11th Day of February 1731/2 about 10 in the Morning & was baptised the 5th of April following Mr Beverley Whiting & Capt. Christopher Brooks Godfathers and Mrs Mildred Gregory Godmother.*
> —Record of George Washington's birth
> in Family Bible

7 Who was George Washington named after?

Not George II of England! Mary Ball Washington gave her firstborn the name of George in honor of Colonel George W. Eskridge, Sr., her guardian before her marriage to Augustine Washington. Eskridge supposedly had come to Virginia as an unwilling indentured servant after having been seized in Wales by a press gang and placed on a ship bound for the colonies. He was sold to a planter, served an indenture of eight years, and finally made his way back to England where he earned a law degree. He returned to Virginia and became a successful attorney in Westmoreland County and a member of the Virginia House of Burgesses.

Had Mary Ball chosen a conventional Washington family name for her firstborn, it probably would have been John, since the other two favorites, Lawrence and Augustine, were already bestowed on George's older half brothers.

8 Where was Washington born?

Washington was born at Popes Creek, in Westmoreland County, Virginia. Later called Wakefield, Popes Creek was part of the Bridges Creek plantation, the original Washington family seat in Virginia. The house at Popes Creek was situated about three-quarters of a mile from the Potomac River, easily visible from the Maryland shoreline. When George was three and a half years old his father moved the family sixty miles up the Potomac to an estate near Little Hunting Creek, known later as Mount Vernon.

Washington often visited Popes Creek during his adolescence. Popes Creek remained in the family of Washington's half brother Augustine, Jr. ("Austin"), until the eve of the Civil War, when it was deeded to the state of Virginia. In 1882 the site, which includes the Washington family cemetery, passed into federal hands, and is now administered by the National Park Service.

9 So George Washington lived at Mount Vernon as a child?

Yes, but not for long. When George was six years old his father decided to move nearer to his iron works on Accokeek Creek, eight miles northwest of Fredericksburg. Augustine, Sr., purchased a plantation on the Rappahannock River outside Fredericksburg, known later as Ferry Farm, in King George (Stafford after 1776) County. After his father's death George often visited his half brother Lawrence at Mount Vernon, and settled there himself after Lawrence's death.

10 How long did Washington live at Ferry Farm?

Until he leased Mount Vernon from his brother's widow, in 1754. Ferry Farm is thus known as Washington's boyhood home and many of the stories of his childhood supposedly took place there, including the tales related by "Parson" Mason Locke Weems.

Comprised of three tracts of land and called "the Home House" by Washington, Ferry Farm also was known as the Strother Farm and Pine Grove. The name Ferry Farm derived from the fact that the family operated a ferry at the riverfront across the Rappahannock.

The house at Ferry Farm caught fire on Christmas Eve 1740 but was repaired and lasted until the 1830s. George inherited Ferry Farm when his father died in 1743, but gave its income to his mother until 1772, when she moved to a house on Charles Street in Fredericksburg. In 1774 Washington sold Ferry Farm to Dr. Hugh Mercer, a Fredericksburg physician and close friend who was killed at the Battle of Princeton in 1777.

11 What about the later history of Ferry Farm?

Federal forces occupied Ferry Farm during the American Civil War and used it as a staging point in the campaigns against Fredericksburg. In 1996 Ferry Farm was acquired by the George Washington Foundation, which also owns Historic Kenmore, the Fredericksburg home of Washington's sister Betty Lewis. Recent archaeological excavations at Ferry Farm uncovered the foundations of the house where Washington lived as a boy.

12 Is it true that Washington never told a lie?

Have you? Or have you not? George Washington was and is known for his character. People of his own time especially thought Washington a man of honor and above reproach. And he was. But that does not mean that Washington was perfect. Although he prided himself on his integrity, Washington, like anyone, was at times forgetful, secretive, capable of self-deception, and susceptible to temptation. He did on occasion attempt to hide the truth—evidenced by the fact that he personally managed American espionage during the Revolutionary War.

13 Did Washington chop down the cherry tree?

This quaint little story is perhaps the most famous of all the tales repeated about George Washington. It is impossible to say or prove that it never happened, but the tone of its source indicates that is was a literary composition fabricated to illustrate to young readers the virtue of honesty, a virtue considered by many to be exemplified in the character and life of Washington. The story first appeared after Washington's death, in the fifth edition of Mason Locke Weems's *Life of Washington* (Augusta, Georgia, 1806).

Weems credited the anecdote of the cherry tree to "an aged lady, who was a distant relative, and, when a girl, spent much of her time in the family" of Washington. If such a lady existed her identity has never been discovered, although Parson Weems did in fact scour the Northern Neck of Virginia in search of stories about Washington. Since Washington's father died when George was only eleven years old, and Washington scarcely mentioned him in all of his correspondence, nothing is known about their relationship. So, while we cannot categorically say the legend is false, we can doubt its credibility as historical fact.

Out of Weems's stories came the tradition that Washington never told a lie.

"Pa, (said George very seriously) do I ever tell lies?"

"No, George, I thank God *you do not, my son; and I rejoice in the hope you never will. At least, you shall never, from me, have cause to be guilty of so shameful a thing. Many parents, indeed, even compel their children to this vile practice, by barbarously beating them for every little fault; hence, on the next offence, the little terrified creature slips out a* lie! *just to escape the rod. But as to yourself, George, you know I have* always *told you, and now tell you again, that, whenever by accident you do any thing wrong, which must often be the case, as you are but a poor little boy yet, without* experience or knowledge, *never tell a falsehood to conceal it; but come* bravely *up, my son, like a* little man, *and tell me of it: and instead of beating you, George, I will but the more honour and love you for it, my dear."*

This, you'll say, was sowing good seed!—Yes, it was: and the crop, thank God, was, as I believe it ever will be, where a man acts the true parent, that is, the Guardian Angel, *by his child.*

The following anecdote is a case in point. *It is too valuable to be lost, and too true to be doubted; for it was communicated to me by the same excellent lady to whom I am indebted for the last.*

When George, said she, was about six years old, he was made the wealthy master of a hatchet! *of which, like most little boys, he was immoderately fond, and was constantly going about chopping every thing that came in his way. One day, in the garden, where he often amused himself hacking his mother's pea-sticks, he unluckily tried the edge of his hatchet on the body of a beautiful young English cherry-tree, which he barked so terribly, that I don't believe the tree ever got the better of it. The next morning the old gentleman finding out what had befallen his tree, which, by the by, was a great favourite, came into the house, and with much warmth asked for the mischievous author, declaring at the same time, that he would not have taken five guineas for his tree. Nobody could tell him any thing about it. Presently George and his hatchet made their appearance. George, said his father,* do you know who killed that beautiful little cherry-tree yonder in the garden? *This was a tough question; and George staggered under it for a moment; but quickly recovered himself: and looking at his father, with the sweet face of youth brightened with the inexpressible charm of all-conquering truth, he bravely cried out,* "I can't tell a lie, Pa; you know I can't tell a lie. I did cut it with my hatchet."—Run to my arms, you dearest boy, *cried his father in transports,* run to my arms; glad am I, George, that you killed my tree; for you have paid me for it a thousand fold. Such an act of heroism in my son, is more worth than a thousand trees, though blossomed with silver, and their fruits of purest gold.

—Mason Locke Weems, *Life of Washington,* 1806

14 Did Washington throw a silver dollar across the Potomac River?

This is a good example of how a plausible and probably true story gets garbled into something that cannot possibly have happened. The original story, told to illustrate Washington's great strength, appeared in George Washington Parke Custis's *Recollections and Private Memoirs of Washington* (Washington, D.C., 1859). Custis was Washington's stepgrandson and the father of Mary Anna Randolph Custis Lee (Robert E. Lee's wife), who edited the *Recollections* from accounts that Custis had written for newspapers before his death in 1857. In a section of the *Recollections* entitled "Washington: His person and personal appearance. Anecdotes of his great physical prowess," a number of stories are related that were remembered by Custis or that had been passed on to him by various people who had known Washington.

While alive, Washington had been known for his great strength, as had his father, Augustine, before him. As early as the French and Indian War both native Virginians and Englishmen remarked on George

Washington's appearance and the way he carried himself. Custis thus related only what was considered common knowledge in late eighteenth-century America when he wrote that, "In person Washington was unique: he looked like no one else. To a stature lofty and commanding, he united a form of the manliest proportions, limbs cast in Nature's finest mould, and a carriage the most dignified, graceful, and imposing. No one ever approached the Pater Patriæ that did not feel his presence." Custis's assertion that an officer of Washington's revolutionary guard often had been heard "to observe, that the Commander-in-Chief was thought to be the strongest man in his army" was not new or unusual. Furthermore, said Custis, exhibitions of Washington's great strength were "apparently attended by scarcely any effort."

Among Custis's anecdotes of his grandfather's strength is the origin of Washington throwing the silver dollar across the Potomac River. "The power of Washington's arm was displayed in several memorable instances—in his throwing a stone across the Rappahannock river below Fredericksburg, another from the bed of the stream to the top of the Natural Bridge, and yet another over the Palisades into the Hudson." Undoubtedly the ability of the young Washington to throw a stone across the river at Ferry Farm, his boyhood home on the Rappahannock River below Fredericksburg, Virginia, was counted as a great feat, and in fact it was.

15 Is it really possible that Washington accomplished the feat?

Yes! The river at Ferry Farm is about two hundred and fifty feet across. In 1936 Fredericksburg officials recruited the renowned professional baseball pitcher Walter Johnson (then retired) of the nearby Washington (National) Senators team to replicate the feat by throwing a silver dollar across the Rappahannock at a point on the river about two hundred and seventy-two feet wide. With some twenty-five hundred spectators standing watch, Johnson's first try fell into the water shy of the opposing riverbank. His second toss sailed a full three hundred and seventeen feet, however, demonstrating that Washington indeed could have achieved a similar result at Ferry Farm.

When the story changed to a silver dollar across the Potomac River is not known. (Clearly by the 1930s, when Walter Johnson accomplished his feat.) Two things are for sure, however. First, neither Washington nor anyone else could throw a rock or a coin across the Potomac River at Mount Vernon, the first president's home. The Potomac is a mile wide at that point. The second fact is, that George Washington was as parsimonious as anyone of his generation, and never for a moment considered throwing away a silver dollar, or a coin of any denomination.

Custis also mentioned that Washington could fling a stone to the top of the Natural Bridge in Virginia. Washington did visit the Natural Bridge when inspecting a chain of French and Indian War forts. The Natural Bridge, owned at one time by Thomas Jefferson, was considered in Washington's day to be one of the two most spectacular natural phenomena in America—the other being Niagara Falls—and its arch is some two hundred and twelve feet, higher than the falls at Niagara. We have it on Washington's own authority that this part of the story is true, for when David Humphrey submitted his manuscript biography of Washington to the president to edit, Washington left the passage unchanged. As for Washington throwing a stone "over the Palisades into the Hudson," Custis presumably meant that Washington was able to hurl a stone from the top of the cliffs outward far enough for it to drop into the water below. The Hudson or New Jersey Palisades range in height from three hundred to five hundred feet.

16 What kind of education did Washington receive?

We are not completely sure. David Humphrey's assertion in his biography of Washington that "his education was principally conducted by a private tutor" must be accepted, because Washington himself edited Humphrey's manuscript and let the statement stand. Likewise, Washington's correspondence indicates that at some point he attended school near the area of his birthplace in Westmoreland County. Unsubstantiated traditions say his first tutor was a sexton in

Truro Parish named Hobby, and that he attended Henry Williams's school near Popes Creek and Reverend James Marye's school in Fredericksburg.

Whatever the sources of Washington's education, they were more than adequate given the illustrious career that followed, although he always considered his education inferior to the formal learning provided to many of his planter and political peers. Had his father lived Washington probably would have been sent to school in England like his two older half brothers and eventually attended college in America or abroad. That was not to be, however, but his surviving school exercises show that he was given a solid preparation for the future. He practiced a good deal of writing, spelling, grammar, and mathematics. Consisting much of copy work and math lessons, Washington was introduced to a variety of subjects, including surveying, geography, poetry, and legal forms.

Washington's formal education, such as it was, ended with an apprenticeship in surveying. His acquisition of knowledge did not, however. As an adult Washington became a voracious reader, eager to keep abreast of the latest developments in politics, agriculture, science, and the arts. He spent hours every day reading correspondence and newspapers from across the country. He also read all the military manuals of his day. His library, eventually numbering more than nine hundred volumes, also included works on philosophy, literature, religion, history, geography, and travel. All this was supplemented by a large number of reference works and maps.

Washington, to his delight, was conferred honorary degrees from several institutions of higher learning, including Harvard College in 1776.

> *Do not forget, that there ought to be a time appropriated to attain this knowledge; as well as to indulge in pleasure. As we now have no opportunities to improve from example, let us read, for this desirable end.*
> —George Washington, Orders, 1756

As president, Washington proposed to Congress the creation of a national university and a military academy. Congress rejected his plan, although the latter was established not long after his death. Washington supported several schools, including Washington College at Chestertown, Maryland; Alexandria Academy in Alexandria, Virginia; and Liberty Hall Academy in Lexington, Virginia (now Washington and Lee University). He also made liberal provisions for educational institutions in his Last Will and Testament. During his lifetime Washington also saw to it that his stepchildren and nephews and nieces were given the opportunity to gain an education—gestures not uniformly appreciated by the recipients.

> *As nothing is of more importance than the education of youth, so consequently nothing can be more laudably beneficial than the association which is formed in Alexandria to effect this desirable purpose. I therefore not only highly approve the institution, but am thankful for the honor done me by enrolling my name among the Managers of it; and as far as it is in my power will give it support.*
> —George Washington to William Brown, 1785

17 What are the Rules of Civility?

The most famous of Washington's school exercises is the "Rules of Civility & Decent Behaviour In Company and Conversation," a list of one hundred and ten decrees intended to assist in instructing the proper social etiquette expected of the Virginia gentry. Once thought to have been Washington's composition because they seemed to be exemplified in his life, many still believe the Rules of Civility were formative in the development of his character.

> *1st Every Action done in Company, ought to be with Some Sign of Respect, to those that are Present....*
> *109th Let your Recreations be Manfull not Sinfull....*
> *110th Labour to keep alive in your Breast that Little*

Spark of Celestial fire Called Conscience.
—Rules of Civility & Decent Behaviour
In Company and Conversation, c.1642,
copied by George Washington, c.1747

18 Did Washington speak a foreign language?

No, although there is some evidence that he may have studied Latin as a youth, and he thought about learning French after the Revolutionary War in preparation of a planned trip to Europe.

19 Did Washington wear a powdered wig?

No. Washington was not a slave to fashion, but then again, he did not ignore it either. He dressed and powdered his reddish-brown hair, as evidenced by eyewitness accounts and records of his purchases. In 1781 Washington ordered six pounds of superfine hair powder and ten balls of blacking, and in 1783 he ordered another ten pounds of "the best Hair powder," four pounds of which was to be gray. In 1782 Washington gave orders to the Continental army to allow every one hundred men two pounds of flour and a half-pound of rendered tallow for dressing the hair.

> *His hair is a little gray & combed smoothly back from the forehead & in a small que—no curls & but very little Powder to it.*
> —British prisoner George Bennet to his mother, 1783

20 Did Washington have wooden teeth?

No! Some have speculated that the discolored condition of Washington's surviving false teeth gave rise to the erroneous belief that they were made of wood.

Despite the fact that George Washington brushed his teeth regularly and had access to the best dental care in America, he began losing his teeth at an early age and by the time he was elected president he had only one natural tooth left. Accordingly, he had at least six pairs of false teeth constructed for his personal use, including sets made by Dr. John Greenwood, the most celebrated dentist in America. Substances used to fabricate the dentures included hippopotamus ivory, gold, animal, and even human teeth.

Washington's poor teeth resulted in routine pain and discomfort as well as illnesses. Although he loved nuts, which ironically may have contributed to some broken teeth—John Adams wrote that Washington lost his teeth by cracking Brazil nuts between his jaws— he relied more and more on soft foods as he grew older. Before he turned to full dentures Washington also attempted to have human teeth, purchased from slaves, transplanted into his mouth. Many have speculated that associated dental pain along with the awkward-fitting dentures resulted in the puffy jaws and generally uncomfortable look displayed in many of Washington's portraits.

21 Did Washington commission Betsy Ross to sew the first American flag?

No, it seems not–despite Ross family tradition. Claims that Betsy sewed the first Star-Spangled Banner at the urging of Washington and a secret committee of Congress that included Robert Morris and her uncle, George Ross, were made by her grandchildren, based on information supposedly related to them by the seamstress and her sister. The story surfaced publicly in a paper delivered by Ross's grandson William Canby in 1870 at a meeting of the Pennsylvania Historical Society.

Canby declared that the three men visited Ross's upholstery shop shortly in late May or early June 1776 with a rough drawing and a request for her to make a flag. His grandmother, said Canby, looked at the drawing and saw "some defects in its proportions and the arrangement and shape of the stars." Ross suggested altering the shape of the flag from a square and changing its six-pointed stars to five points. The committee agreed, so the account goes, and Washington made a new drawing that the committee carried back to Congress, where it was approved.

The gentlemen of the committee and General Washington very respectfully considered the suggestions and acted upon them, General Washington seating himself at a table with a pencil and paper, altered the drawing and then made a new one according to the suggestions of my mother [Betsy Ross]. That General Washington seemed to her to be the active one in making the design, the others having little or nothing to do with it.
—Rachel Fletcher, Affidavit, 1871

The problem with the Betsy Ross story is that there is no evidence to support it, neither in the voluminous papers of Washington nor those of Congress, nor in Ross's own papers. Washington was in Philadelphia for three or four days at the beginning of June 1776, it is true, but no evidence has yet surfaced indicating that he had time to think about flag designs. Betsy Ross did make flags and she received a payment for making a flag from the Pennsylvania State Navy Board, a year later, in 1777. But there is no overlap between Betsy's flag and George Washington.

The Continental Congress resolved to create a national flag in 1777, on 14 June—now celebrated as Flag Day. Many believe that poet and artist Francis Hopkinson, a Signer of the Declaration of Independence, designed the flag that was then adopted, for he submitted a bill in 1780 for designing "the flag of the United States of America." There arose much contention among some of the delegates in Congress about paying the bill, but no one at the time ever denied Hopkinson's assertion that he designed the flag.

Resolved. That the flag of the United States be thirteen stripes, alternate red and white; that the union be thirteen stars, white in a blue field, representing a new constellation.
—Resolution of Congress, 1777

22 How tall was George Washington?

Six feet, three and one-half inches "exact" is what Washington measured in death, according to Tobias Lear, who ordered his coffin. George Mercer wrote in 1760 that Washington was six feet, two inches, tall in 1759 when he took his seat in the Virginia House of Burgesses. Washington routinely ordered clothes for a man six feet tall, so we must assume that his height was somewhere in between. In any case, he was much taller than the average person of his age.

23 How much did Washington weigh?

According to a 1760 description written by George Washington's friend and fellow French and Indian War officer, George Mercer, Washington weighed 175 pounds in 1759. The last time Washington stepped on the scales, in 1799, according to his stepgrandson George Washington Parke Custis, Washington weighed "a little rising 210." Custis also quotes Washington as saying that the "best weight of his best days never exceeded from 210 to 220."

24 Did Washington lack a sense of humor, or was he what we would call a stick in the mud?

No, he was subtle and spontaneous, yet quite guarded. It seems there is a widespread view of the first president as a humorless, dour old goat who enjoyed frowning more than anything else in life. One observer said that Washington had only "a little bit of a sense of humor," and his best biographer, the great historian and author Douglas Southall Freeman, went so far as to say that George Washington exhibited "no spontaneous sense of humor and while he occasionally indulged a laugh, it was over a bit of horseplay or some ludicrous harmless accident." Not ringing endorsements, by any means.

Washington may have not been a Red Skelton or Lucille Ball, but such observations surely would have surprised him. Since Freeman's day, others, attempting to understand the internal man, have developed more nuanced interpretations of Washington. These observers notice a private side of Washington that was apparent to his inner circle of family and close friends—but consciously hidden in his public persona, especially after taking control of the Continental army, and even more so after being elected president.

> *It is assuredly better to go laughing than crying thro'*
> *the rough journey of life*
> —George Washington to Theodorick Bland, 1786

Those looking at the more obscure side of Washington have described his sense of humor as subtle, ironic, wry, fine, natural, amusing, well-developed, tremendous, strong, pronounced, tart, caustic, earthy, and even wicked. He liked to hear and repeat jokes, especially those with witty punch lines. His letters and diary entries and surviving anecdotes of his contemporaries attest to a subtle and spontaneous sense of humor.

Washington appreciated amusing situations and the subjects of his humor were varied: military life, blundering subordinates, invitations to dinner, poetry written in his honor, sitting for portraits, money, false teeth, love, marriage, and births. Contemporary accounts abound that portray Washington as laughing "very heartily," with "infinite glee," and "till the tears ran down his eyes." Chief Justice John Marshall said that Washington "actually rolled on the ground in merriment" when Marshall related how he and Bushrod Washington (Washington's nephew and another Supreme Court Justice) had lost their clothes while bathing in the Potomac.

One instance took place in Philadelphia when Washington was president. Washington attended the theater where the comedy "Old Soldier" was playing. (Washington loved the theater and especially comedies.) The central character, "Darby," was a buffoonish veteran of the Continental army who gave an exaggerated impression of General Washington. "All eyes in the theater turned toward the presidential box to witness Washington's hearty laugh," a Philadelphia newspaper reported the next day.

Mark Twain, upon learning of a report of his death in 1897, quipped, "The report of my death was an exaggeration." Compare that to Washington's statement, one hundred and forty years earlier, written to his brother after the Battle of Monongahela in 1755. "The report of my death was an exaggeration," wrote Washington. "As I heard since my arrivl at this place, a circumstantial account of my death and dying Speech, I take this early opportunity of contradicting the first, and of assuring you that I have not, as yet, composed the latter."

Or consider Washington's 1762 letter to a brother-in-law, chiding him for writing letters on Sunday morning, "when you ought to have been at Church, praying as becomes every good Christian Man who has as much to answer for as you have." Washington then went on to accuse his correspondent of sitting around "lost in admiration" of a newborn child while neglecting "your Crops &c.—pray how will this be reconciled to that anxious care and vigilance, which is so escencially necessary at a time when our growing Property—meaning the Tobacco—is assailed by every villainous worm that has had an existence since the days of Noah (how unkind it was of Noah now I have mentioned his name to suffer such a brood of Vermin to get a birth in the Ark) but perhaps you may be as well of[f] as we are—that is, have no Tobacco for them to eat and there I think we nicked the Dogs, as I think to do you if you expect any more." Humorous in its entirety, this letter was labeled a forgery by Freeman, who did not have access to it, because it seemed to him out of character for Washington.

25 Are there other examples of Washington's sense of humor?

Yes, many. A 1786 letter to a neighbor concerning the failure of Royal Gift, the Spanish jackass sent to Washington by the king of Spain, to perform stud service according to expectations, provides a good example of Washington's humor. "Particular attention shall be paid to the Mares which your Servant brought," Washington wrote, "and when my Jack is in the humour they shall derive all the benefits of his labours—for labour it appears to be. At present, tho' young, he follows what one may suppose to be the example of his late royal master, who cannot, tho' past his grand climacterick, perform seldomer, or with more majestic solemnity, than he does. However, I am not without hope, that when he becomes a little better acquainted with republican enjoyments, he will amend his manners, and fall into a better & more expeditious mode of doing business. If the case should be otherwise, I should have no disinclination to present his Catholic majesty with as good a thing, as he gave me."

To another neighbor who sent his jenny to Mount Vernon for a like purpose, Washington wrote, "I feel myself much obliged by your polite offer of the first fruits of your Jenny. Tho' in appearance quite unequal to the match—yet, like a true female, she was not to be terrified at the disproportionate size of her paramour." To Royal Gift's credit, he eventually did produce offspring with a jenny belonging to Washington.

Similar in kind was Washington's remark about a Revolutionary War colonel getting married in old age and needing to check his "ammunition, etc." And when he learned that the Marquis de Chastellux was to be married, he wrote to the Frenchman, who had served in America as a major general, "I can hardly refrain from smiling to find you caught at last. . . . now you are well served for coming to fight in favor of the American rebels, all the way across the Atlantic ocean, by catching that terrible contagion—domestic felicity—which same, like smallpox, a man can have only once in his life."

Washington wrote in his diary of a notoriously lazy overseer, that he was, "hard at work with an ax—very extraordinary this." Likewise, upon attending a German Reformed Church in York, Pennsylvania, in 1791, Washington confided in his diary, "Received, and answered an address from the Inhabitants of York town—& there being no Episcopal Minister present in the place, I went to hear morning Service performed in the Dutch reformed Church—which, being in that language not a word of which I understood I was in no danger of becoming a proselyte to its religion by the eloquence of the Preacher."

Upon learning of the duel in 1798 between Federalist James Jones and Republican H. Brockholst Livingston in New York, Washington remarked, "They say the shot Jones fired at his opponent cut a piece off his nose. How could he miss it? You know Mr. Livingston's nose and what a capitol target it is."

Typical of the anecdotes that circulated after Washington's death is one told by William Thornton, the architect of the United States Capitol: "As he sat at table after dinner," recalled Thornton, "the fire behind him was too large and hot. He complained, and said he must remove. A gentleman observed it behooved the General to stand fire. 'Yes, said Washington, but it does not look well for a General to receive the fire behind.'"

The list of similar anecdotes and quotations regarding Washington's sense of humor could be extended indefinitely.

26 Did Washington have a terrible temper?

Yes, but a well-controlled wrath that he learned early to control, even when greatly agitated. Thomas Jefferson followed his famous description of Washington as "a wise, a good, and a great man" with the observation that "His temper was naturally high toned; but reflection and resolution had obtained a firm and habitual ascendency over it. If ever, however, it broke its bonds, he was most tremendous in his wrath."

No doubt, Washington's self-control was learned over time. When he was sixteen years old a fellow Virginian told his mother that George was "subject to attacks of anger and provocation, sometimes without just cause." There is a story that shows the truth of this observation: as a young man he lost his temper and wrongly insulted a fellow in public in Williamsburg, who in turn knocked him down. Washington thought about the matter and decided he had been mistaken, and apologized.

> *105th Be not Angry at Table whatever happens & if you have reason to be so, Shew it not but on a Chearfull Countenance especially if there be Strangers for Good Humour makes one Dish of Meat a Feast.*
> —Rules of Civility & Decent Behaviour
> In Company and Conversation, c.1642,
> copied by George Washington, c.1747

Perhaps the most blatant example of Washington's wrath in his own writings is contained in his letter to George Muse, a captain in the Virginia Regiment during the French and Indian War who while intoxicated wrote an indiscreet letter to Washington complaining about his share of land bounty grants. Washington told Muse that he was "not accustomed to receive such from any Man, nor would have taken the same language from you personally, without letting you feel some marks of my resentment; I would advise you to be cautious in writing me a second of the same tenour." Washington also complained about having "ever engag'd in behalf of so ungrateful & dirty a fellow as you are" and concluded that he was sorry he ever "took the trouble of mentioning the Land, or your name in a Letter, as I do not think you merit the least assistance from G: Washington."

Examples of Washington's anger survive from the Revolutionary War. The most famous is that he cursed when he saw Major General Charles Lee retreating at the Battle of Monmouth Courthouse in June 1778. When asked whether he had ever heard Washington swear, Brigadier General Charles Scott answered, "Yes, sir, he did once. It was at Monmouth and on a day that would have made any man swear. Yes, sir, he swore that day till the leaves shook on the trees. Charming! Delightful! Never have I enjoyed such swearing before or since. Sir, on that memorable day he swore like an angel from heaven!" Scott's observation came long after the battle and was related second hand, and whether Washington really cursed has been disputed by serious scholarship, but not the fact that Washington was extremely angry. Perhaps he was most furious at Benedict Arnold after his treason, although any potential outburst was prevented by Arnold's successful evasion of capture.

During the presidency, in 1791, Washington was sent word of the Indian victory over Arthur St. Clair's army on the Wabash River near present-day Fort Recovery, Ohio, then in the Northwest Territory. (The lands west of Pennsylvania and northwest of the Ohio River, that is, present-day Ohio, Indiana, Michigan, Illinois, Wisconsin, and northeast Minnesota.) When the news arrived Washington was at dinner. He was called away, heard the news, and returned to the table as if nothing had happened. He then attended a group of ladies at a reception, greeting each in turn. After the visitors had taken their leave Washington shook with violent emotion and let loose a series of choice words. According to his secretary, Washington "threw his hands up as he hurled imprecations upon St. Clair." But finally he gained his composure and declared that he would hear St. Clair "without prejudice."

Displays of Washington's fierce temper at Edmund Randolph, Philip Freneau, and even Alexander Hamilton are all without doubt. Once he even exploded during a cabinet meeting.

> *The President was much inflamed, got into one of those passions when he cannot command himself, ran on much on the personal abuse which has been bestowed on him, defied any man on earth to produce one single act of his since he had been in the govmt which was not done on the purest motives, that he had never repented but once the having slipped the moment of resigning his office, & that was every moment since, that* by god *he had rather be in his grave than in his present situation. That he had rather be on his farm than to be made* emperor of the world *and yet they were charging him with wanting to be a king.*
>
> —Thomas Jefferson, The Anas, 1793

27 How did Washington get his start?

Washington began life with some advantages, as his father had left him Ferry Farm plantation and a dozen or so slaves. His education, though limited by some standards, was sufficient to set him on the path to becoming a surveyor, which in the eighteenth century was a profession that offered boundless opportunities for an enterprising young man like Washington. George's half brother Lawrence opened doors for his younger brother with the prominent Fairfax family of Belvoir—Lawrence's inlaws—including Thomas, Lord Fairfax, who's Northern Neck Proprietary consisted of more than five million acres. Lord Fairfax provided plenty of work for his young friend and gave him ample opportunity to scope out some fine lands for himself. Just as important, the Fairfax connection brought recognition to Washington from the colony's first circles, leading to his being commissioned the first surveyor of Culpeper County in 1749 by the president and masters of the College of William and Mary, the authorities responsible for issuing surveyorships.

28 Did his mother stop Washington from joining the British Navy?

Yes. In the summer of 1746 George's half brother Lawrence tried to persuade his stepmother, Mary Ball Washington, that young George's future lay at sea. Mary wrote to her own half brother, Joseph Ball, asking for his advice. Ball wrote back from England advising against it, saying that fourteen-year-old George "had better be put apprentice to a Tinker" than be sent to sea, where "they will . . . Cut him & Slash him and use him like a Negro, or rather, like a Dog." Mary apparently put her foot down about the matter, the idea was abandoned and George stayed in Virginia.

29 Was Washington the richest man in America?

No, and he would have been surprised to hear it! Washington did have great personal wealth by most standards, although much of it was tied up in western lands that would never benefit him personally. In fact, those lands were a continual drain on both his resources and his time. He lived in a period when the economy was not cash based, and in Washington's case he was often unsure whether he was even solvent or not. In the late 1760s and early 1770s, he owed money to British merchants and regularly robbed Peter to pay Paul. Despite his best efforts, Washington was unable to manage his financial affairs from afar during the Revolutionary War, being able to briefly visit Mount Vernon only while en route to and from Yorktown. His constant financial struggles left him cash poor, so much so that by the time he left to take the office of the presidency in 1789 he had to borrow money to make the trip.

Washington kept detailed and accurate financial records, and his correspondence is replete with financial concerns. So far, no attempt has been made to chronicle and assess Washington's financial history. However, it is plain that others of his era accumulated (and in some cases lost!) more wealth than Washington. His eighty thousand acres of land, for instance, pales in comparison to the millions of acres owned in New York by members of the Livingston and Van Rensselaer families or the five million acres held in Virginia by Thomas, Lord Fairfax. Other wealthy persons of the time include: Jacob Bacon of Woodbury, Connecticut, a store merchant said to be a millionaire as early as 1750; Charles Carroll of Carrollton, a Maryland planter; William Duer, a land speculator of New York; and Robert Morris of Philadelphia, the Financier of the Revolution.

In his Last Will and Testament, Washington estimated the value of his total estate to be about $530,000, a significant sum of course, but hardly the largest in the country.

30 What did Washington do for fun?

Washington had several hobbies and amusements that he engaged in over the course of most of his life. They included foxhunting, card playing, dancing, horse racing, and the theater. His foxhunting escapades usually included neighboring planters or visitors and often the hunts were followed by dinner at Mount Vernon and an evening of cards. When Washington played cards or attended horse races he typically waged small amounts of money, faithfully recording his meager winnings or losses in his account books. George and Martha often went to balls, and he was known to spend an entire evening dancing with all the ladies in attendance, staying as late as 2:00 A.M. When he was younger Washington frequented cockfights, which were still popular in Virginia, and during the presidency he patronized the circus and museums.

Washington's favorite pastime may have been going to the theater. Before the Revolutionary War, he and Martha made it a point to attend every play that was performed in nearby Alexandria. The practice continued, when possible, during the war, and during the presidency while they were living in New York and Philadelphia. The first performance that Washington seems to have attended took place when he and his half brother Lawrence traveled to Barbados in 1751. In Barbados, the brothers saw George Lillo's *The London Merchant, or the History of George Barnwell*. His favorite play was Joseph Addison's *Cato: A Tragedy*, performances of which he attended numerous times. Washington often referred to scenes from plays in his writings.

Washington also genuinely enjoyed reading and learning about agriculture and scientific advances and novelties of the day.

31 Did Washington like animals?

Yes. As a farmer, soldier, hunter, and frequenter of horse races, Washington took a special interest in animals. He bred horses, priding himself on the quality of his stock, which he routinely traded and sold. He also raised mules and donkeys, which he thought more efficient than horses for farm work. He raised oxen, swine, cattle, sheep, and chickens, as well, and was keen to notice the livestock of other farmers wherever he went. Likewise, Washington bred several kinds of dogs, especially hounds, which he used for hunting and protecting the livestock and crops at Mount Vernon.

Washington's friends and acquaintances often sent him animals, including horses, jackasses, sheep, dogs, and birds. After the Revolution, Lafayette sent him two jennets, a jackass, French hounds, and a golden pheasant. Washington likewise gave animals to his relatives and friends. As president, Washington was intrigued by artist Charles Willson Peale's museum of natural history in Philadelphia, with its extensive collection of fish, birds, reptiles, and exotic animals. Washington even donated to the museum the golden pheasant given to him by Lafayette.

> *I have just had the satisfaction, with a number of gentlemen, of viewing a remarkably large fat ox, which has been presented by some gentlemen in Connecticut to his Excellency General Washington. He is six feet seven inches high, and weighs on the hoof three thousand five hundred pounds, the largest animal I ever beheld.*
> —James Thatcher, Journal entry, 1779

28

32 Is it true that Washington was the finest horseman of his age?

Maybe so, at least that's what Thomas Jefferson said, in 1816, in an oft-quoted recollection: "His person, you know, was fine, his stature exactly what one would wish, his deportment easy, erect and noble; the best horseman of his age, and the most graceful figure that could be seen on horseback."

> *I have been much gratified this day with a view of General Washington. His excellency was on horseback, in company with several military gentlemen. It was not difficult to distinguish him from all others; his personal appearance is truly noble and majestic; being tall and well proportioned. His dress is a blue coat with buff-colored facings, a rich epaulette on each shoulder, buff under dress, and an elegant small sword; a black cockade in his hat.*
> —James Thatcher, Journal entry, 1775

George Washington Parke Custis also recalled that Washington near the end of his life had retained all the physical powers of his youth, and that "those powers became rather mellowed than decayed by time, for 'his age was like a lusty winter, frosty yet kindly,' and, up to his sixty-eighth year, he mounted a horse with surprising agility, and rode with the ease and gracefulness of his better days."

One thing is for certain, Washington liked horses, and horse racing, and bought, traded, and bred horses over the course of his whole life. During the Revolutionary War, he had several mounts ready at all times, including some now famous, Blueskin and Nelson. Once during the Revolutionary War, his aide-de-camp wrote that Washington had been in the saddle for more than twenty-four hours. Thirteen horses conveyed Washington to the Southern states during his presidential tour: a white parade steed, Prescott, that Washington mounted for ceremonial purposes along the way, and four each for his coach, baggage wagon, and escort. In his retirement at Mount Vernon, Washington spent several hours a day riding about his plantations.

Eighteenth- and nineteenth-century artists liked to depict horses in their paintings and sculptures of Washington. One of Washington's studhorses, Traveller, lent its name to Robert E. Lee's famous wartime mount, hitherto called Jefferson Davis.

> *His movements and gestures are graceful, his walk majestic, and he is a splendid horseman.*
> —George Mercer, 1760

Washington's body servant during the Revolution, William "Billy" Lee, usually accompanied his master on foxhunts. According to George Washington Parke Custis, Lee "rode a horse called *Chinkling*, a surprising leaper, and very much like its rider, low, but sturdy, and of great bone and muscle. Will had but one order, which was to keep with the hounds; and, mounted on *Chinkling*, a French horn at his back, throwing himself almost at length on the animal as with his spur in flank, this fearless horseman would rush, at full speed, through brake or tangled wood, in a style at which modern huntsmen would stand aghast."

33 Is it true that Washington introduced the mule to America?

No, mules were bred in the English colonies long before George Washington was born. The idea that Washington had been responsible for their introduction arose from the newspaper advertisements that he often placed to rent out jackasses for stud service. During the Revolutionary War, Washington became convinced that mules were superior draft animals to horses and even oxen and decided to obtain a Spanish jackass—considered the world's finest—with which to breed mules at Mount Vernon.

King Charles III of Spain and the marquis de Lafayette both sent pairs of jacks to Washington, although only one of each pair lived through the rough sea voyages to America. The survivors, named respectively Royal Gift and Knight of Malta, were bred with twenty of Mount Vernon's best mares, and were rented out to cover mares and jennies from neighboring plantations. The result, in Washington's words, was a race of mules of "extraordinary goodness." On the eve of Washington's death there were more than fifty mules at Mount Vernon.

> *A JACK-ASS of the first race in the kingdom of Spain, will cover mares and Jonnies (she asses) at Mount Vernon the ensuing spring.—The first for Ten, the latter for Fifteen Pounds the season.—Royal Gift is four years old, is between 14-1/2 and 15 hands high, and will grow, it is said, till he is 20 or 25 years of age.—He is very boney and stout made, of a dark colour, with light belly and legs.—The advantages, which are many, to be derived from the propagation of asses from this animal (the first of the kind that ever was in North America) and the usefulness of mules, bred from a Jack of his size, either for the road or team, are well known to those who are acquainted with this mongrel race.—For the information of those who are not, it may be enough to add, that their great strength, longevity, hardiness, and cheap support, give them a preference of horses that is scarcely to be imagined.*

> —Advertisement for Royal Gift
> in *The Virginia Journal* and
> *Alexandria Advertiser*, 1786.

34 Why did Washington make his home at Mount Vernon?

Mainly because it was the finest piece of real estate owned by his family. When his father Augustine moved his family there in 1735, the Virginia colony was still expanding up the rivers from the Chesapeake Bay. The future lay in the west, as Augustine and his sons after him were well aware of, and the land of the Mount Vernon plantations was not worn out from successive generations of farming. Its location, near both Belvoir, the seat of the family that owned the Fairfax Proprietary, and Alexandria, one of Virginia's main commercial centers, meant that the potential for profit at Mount Vernon was nearly unlimited.

35 What is the origin of the name Mount Vernon?

The estate is named after Vice Admiral Edward Vernon, Lawrence Washington's former naval commander, a highly regarded British military hero. Lawrence is usually credited with having suggested the name to his father in 1742. Sitting high above the Potomac River, Washington thought Mount Vernon the most "pleasantly situated" estate in America.

36 When did Washington inherit Mount Vernon?

George Washington inherited Mount Vernon in 1761, after the death of the heirs of his half brother Lawrence Washington. Lawrence had built the house after inheriting the plantation at the death of their father in 1743. The farm consisted of 2,126 acres. Washington did not inherit Mount Vernon directly upon Lawrence's death in 1752, as it was supposed to go to Lawrence's only surviving child, Sarah. At Sarah's death in 1754 Washington rented the life rights from Lawrence's widow Ann Fairfax, and her new husband, George Lee, and upon Ann's death George Washington inherited the property outright under the terms of Lawrence's will.

37 How long did Washington live at Mount Vernon?

Mount Vernon was Washington's home for his entire adult life, and the home to which he brought his bride, Martha, in 1759. He was absent from home, of course, for most of eight years during the Revolutionary War, and for lengthy periods of each year during his two presidential administrations.

Over the decades Washington made substantial improvements to the Mount Vernon estate. After the Revolutionary War he enlarged the house from a small building of eight rooms into a commodious two-story mansion of more than a dozen rooms and passageways, ninety-six feet long by thirty-two feet in depth, complete with a large attic and cellar, a portico, and a columned piazza. He made improvements to the gardens and grounds around the house, sowing the lawn with English grass seeds, planting hedges, replacing dead trees in the serpentine walks and shrubberies, and establishing orchards in the outlying farms.

38 Was Mount Vernon a large plantation?

Yes, if you think of eight thousand acres as large. Actually, Mount Vernon consisted of five plantations plus some outlying tracts, and three mills. At its center was the Mansion House farm, where Washington lived. The other farms were the Union farm, the Dogue Run farm, the Muddy Hole farm, and the River farm.

> I can truly say, I had rather be at Mount Vernon, with a friend or two about me, than to be attended, at the Seat of Government, by the Officers of State, and the Representatives of every Power in Europe.
> —George Washington to David Stuart, 1790

39 What about Mount Vernon's later history?

When George Washington died he left Mount Vernon to his nephew, Justice Bushrod Washington. Bushrod, like his uncle, had no children of his own, and left Mount Vernon at his death in 1829 to his nephew John Augustine Washington, who in turn left it to his widow Jane Charlotte Blackburn Washington at his death in 1832. When

Charlotte died Mount Vernon passed to her son, also named John Augustine Washington (a great-grandson of George Washington's brother John Augustine), who offered the estate to the United States government in 1847. The government declined to purchase the property, however.

In 1860, after years of neglect, the mansion house and two hundred acres were purchased by The Mount Vernon Ladies' Association of the Union, a society chartered in 1856 for the purpose of saving and preserving Mount Vernon. Led by Ann Pamela Cunningham, an invalid from South Carolina, the Ladies' Association raised the funds necessary to buy and begin restoration, and since then has cared for Mount Vernon for almost one hundred and fifty years without any help from either the federal or state governments.

Mount Vernon was designated a National Historic Landmark in 1960. Open to the public every day of the year, including holidays, the Mount Vernon Estate and Gardens include the mansion house, slave quarters, kitchen, stables, greenhouse, flower and vegetable gardens, English boxwoods, a recreation of Washington's sixteen-sided treading barn, and the family and slave burial grounds. Recently a $110 million museum and educational center was added to the property.

40 Why was Washington known as America's First Farmer?

Washington was first a planter and then a soldier and politician, and thought of himself as such. His voluminous diaries are actually agricultural daybooks that contain detailed records of his farming practices, of the weather, and of various agricultural experiments. He was acutely interested in scientific advancements in crop and animal husbandry, and read every pamphlet on the subjects that he could acquire. He habitually corresponded with other planters and leading agriculturists, with whom he exchanged information, plants, and seeds.

Washington's scientific pursuit of agriculture was intellectual but also practical and economical. He was one of the first Virginia planters to abandon tobacco production in favor of wheat, which allowed him to use his lands more efficiently; his superfine flour became known as the best in the colonies. Washington also cultivated other grains, including corn, oats, barley, and rye, as well as hay, alfalfa, various vegetables, hemp, and vines. After the Revolutionary War Washington experimented with crop rotation, using a complex system that extended over seven years and that left all his cropland fallow at some point. Washington also designed and built a two-story, sixteen-sided threshing barn (recently reconstructed at Mount Vernon), allowing the threshing process to take place in all kinds of weather, as well as a dung repository to assist in the manufacture and storage of fertilizer.

As president, Washington unsuccessfully urged Congress to establish a National Board of Agriculture to collect and disseminate information about agriculture—an idea not implemented until Lincoln's administration. Granddaughter Nelly Custis told a friend after Washington's retirement from the presidency, that, "grandpapa is very well and much pleased with being once more Farmer Washington." Visitors to Mount Vernon often echoed Nelly's assessment of her grandfather.

> *I rose early and took a walk about the General's grounds—which are really beautifully laid out. He has about 4000 acres well cultivated and superintends the whole himself. Indeed his greatest pride now is, to be thought the first farmer in America.*
> —John Hunter, Diary entry, 1785

41 Did Washington drink alcohol?

Lots, although no one ever recorded witnessing him inebriated. Alcoholic beverages played a prominent role in the public sphere in colonial America, and Washington offered no resistance to the prevailing trends. When his name was put forward for public office in Virginia he treated the electorate, as was the custom, to copious amounts of beer, rum, punch, wine, cider, and brandy. During both the French and Indian and Revolutionary Wars, Washington made it a point to provide regular rations of rum to the troops, along with orders against drunkenness. Wine also was a staple at the dinner tables of both the Continental army headquarters and the presidential mansion. Washington also frequently partook of alcoholic beverages in public settings, and many accounts survive of his participating in celebratory toasts at various functions.

As a farmer, Washington sometimes bartered part of his flour and herring yields for rum and spirits, and he joined with neighbors in agricultural ventures aimed at establishing viable vineyards in Virginia. He even once sold a runaway slave to the West Indies with directions that the revenue from the sale be used for a hogshead of the best rum, some molasses and sweetmeats, and the "residue, much or little, in good old Spirits."

Washington routinely took a glass of his favorite, Madeira wine, after dinner. Surviving in his papers is a recipe for making thirty gallons of "Small Beer" from boiled "Bran Hops" and molasses, and countless orders to England for various alcoholic beverages, including single orders of up to one hundred and fifty gallons of Madeira. Martha Washington's cookbook contained recipes for making a variety of wines, including cherry, lemon, blackberry, and gooseberry, as well as hippocras, a cordial drink consisting of wine and spices that was the rage in the eighteenth century. Washington also used wines and distilled spirits for medicinal purposes.

> *We cleaned ourselves (to get Rid of the Game we had catched the Night before) & took a Review of the Town & then return'd to our Lodgings where we had a good Dinner prepar'd for us Wine & Rum Punch in Plenty & a good Feather Bed with clean Sheets which was a very agreeable regale.*
> —George Washington, Journal of My Journey Across the Mountains, 1748

42 Did Washington make liquor on his plantation?

Yes. In fact, the stone house with its "five Stills, Boilers—&ca" was one of the most productive distilleries in the country, and it proved to be one of Washington's most lucrative cash businesses. In its best year, Washington's distilling business produced some twelve thousand gallons of whiskey, earning him seventy-five hundred dollars, a handsome sum. Unfortunately for Washington, he died before the distillery had been long in operation. In recent years Mount Vernon has reconstructed Washington's distillery and begun to distill and sell liquor based on Washington's recipe for rye whiskey.

43 Did Washington smoke tobacco?

Apparently not, except when smoking the peace pipe while treating with Indian chiefs. Nor is there any evidence that he chewed tobacco or dipped snuff.

44 Did Washington grow or smoke marijuana?

Gullible, gullible, gullible. Wishing it does not make it so. Neither does saying so, even if you repeat it over and over and over. No, despite the misguided claims of many, Washington never grew nor smoked marijuana. Why would he, after all, when he had unlimited access to opium? Washington did grow hemp, however, as did many colonists of his era—a practice required of Virginia planters by the Virginia House of Burgesses in 1632, and rewarded by bounty in 1722.

By Washington's time the European cultivation of hemp had been taking place for centuries and the properties of the plant were well known. Industrial uses of hemp included the production of rope, oakum, paper, cloth, and fuel. Planted and harvested differently than marijuana, the cultivation of hemp in the eighteenth-century was a labor-intensive process requiring repeated plowing and composting with well-rotted manure. The product, too, was different. Marijuana contains a psychoactive chemical THC (tetrahydrocannabinol) that produces a narcotic effect. Hemp not only has very low THC content but a high amount of an anti-psychoactive ingredient, CBD (cannabinol), which blocks intoxication. The cross-fertilization of marijuana and hemp, in fact, results in the diminution of the THC content in the marijuana.

Washington sowed hemp in 1765, 1766, and 1767 but the resulting harvests were so disappointing that he discontinued the practice. Experiments in the early 1790s with a variety of East India hemp also proved unsuccessful.

45 Was Washington artistic?

Yes, but he was not a portrait or landscape painter, nor did he work in wood or marble, but the many maps drawn by Washington when he was a surveyor show that he did have artistic talents.

46 Did Washington play a musical instrument?

By his own admission, Washington could neither sing "nor raise a single note on any instrument." But he did like music, as attested by his love of balls and dancing. He engaged a music master to give lessons at Mount Vernon to his stepchildren, Patsy and Jacky Custis, and his stepgranddaughter, Nelly Custis. For them he bought a spinet, a violin, a German flute, a harpsichord, and an English guitar.

We are told of the amazing powers of musick in ancient times; but the stories of its effects are so surprising that we are not obliged to believe them, unless they had been founded upon better authority than Poetic assertion—for the Poets of old (whatever they may do in these days) were strangely addicted to the marvellous; and if I before doubted the truth of their relations with respect to the power of musick, I am now fully convinced of their falsity—because I would not, for the honor of my Country, allow that we are left by the Ancients at an immeasurable distance in everything;

and if they could sooth the ferocity of wild beasts—could draw the trees & the stones after them—and could even charm the powers of Hell by their musick, I am sure that your productions would have had at least virtue enough in them (without the aid of voice or instrument) to soften the Ice of the Delaware & Potomack—and in that case you should have had an earlier acknowledgment of your favor of the 1st of December which came to hand but last Saturday.

I readily admit the force of your distinction between "a thing done and a thing to be done"—and as I do not believe that you would do "a very bad thing indeed" I must even make a virtue of necessity, and defend your performance, if necessary, to the last effort of my musical abilities.

But, my dear Sir, if you had any doubts about the reception which your work would meet with—or had the smallest reason to think that you should need any assistance to defend it—you have not acted with your usual good Judgment in the choice of a Coadjuter; for, should the tide of prejudice not flow in favor of it (and so various are the tastes, opinions & whims of men, that even the sanction of Divinity does not ensure universal concurrence) what, alass! can I do to support it? I can neither sing one of the songs, nor raise a single note on any instrument to convince the unbelieving. But I have, however, one argument which will prevail with persons of true taste (at least in America)—I can tell them that it is the production of Mr Hopkinson.

—George Washington to
Francis Hopkinson, 1789

47 Was Washington a member of the Ohio Company?

No, although his half brothers Lawrence and Augustine, along with a handful of prominent Virginians and Englishmen, were founding members. Washington surveyed lands along tributaries of the Potomac River for the company in 1749 or 1750, and it was in part to protect the interests of the company that Virginia Governor Robert Dinwiddie (himself a member of the company) sent Washington to warn off the French in 1753. That trip led to the French and Indian War, and many of the land bounty grants awarded to officers of the Virginia Regiment were in lands originally claimed by the company.

> *I am not a member of, nor am I in any manner, interested in the affairs of the Ohio Company, nor indeed do I know at this time, of whom it consists.*
> —George Washington to Thomas Cresap, 1786

48 Who was the "Low Land Beauty" that infatuated Washington?

By all accounts, it was Lucy Grymes, who married Major General Henry Lee II of Leesylvania in Prince William County, Virginia. Lucy's family was prominent in Richmond County, the county adjacent to Westmoreland where Washington was born and often visited during his youth. Like many in the neighborhood of the Northern Neck, Washington was dazzled by the attractive girl, two years his junior. Whether he made overtures to her or not, and if so whether she ever reciprocated, is not known.

Lucy was a granddaughter of Virginia Governor Edmund Jennings and a grandniece of Richard Lee, the Scholar, one of the colony's most influential persons, and thus when she married Henry Lee she was marrying a not-to-distant relation. Lucy's eight children included Henry, Jr. ("Light-Horse Harry"), Revolutionary War hero and Virginia governor and close friend of Washington, Charles Lee, appointed United States attorney general by Washington and Supreme Court Justice by John Adams, and Richard Bland Lee, a United States congressmen.

While Washington was smitten with Lucy he visited Belvoir, the seat of the Fairfax family, and spent time with Mary Cary, a sister of Sally Fairfax, who somewhat eased the painful memory of his failure to win the Low Land Beauty.

> *My Place of Residence is at present at his Lordships where I might was my heart disengag'd pass my time very pleasantly as theres a very agreeable Young Lady Lives in the same house (Colo. George Fairfax's Wife's sister) but as thats only adding Fuel to fire it makes me the more uneasy for by often and unavoidably being in Company with her revives my former Passion for your Low Land Beauty whereas was I to live more retired from yound Women I might in some measure eliviate my sorrows by burying that chast and troublesome Passion in the grave of oblivion or etarnall forgetfulness for as I am very well assured that's the only antidote or remedy that I ever shall be releivd by or only recess than can administer any cure or help to me as I am well convinced was I ever to attempt any thing I should only get a denial which would be only adding grief to uneasiness.*
> —George Washington to Robin, c.1749

49 What about Sally Fairfax?

Ah, the Lady of Belvoir, the wife of one of Washington's best friends, George William Fairfax. Did Washington fall in love with her? Did she fall in love with Washington? If so, did they let their feelings for one another lead to any physical consummation? Was it just infatuation? Or is it all much ado about nothing? These are questions that have been excitedly debated every since a cryptic letter from the youthful Washington to Sarah Cary Fairfax, written from the frontier during the French and Indian War in September 1758, surfaced in the 1870s.

The controversial letter is clearly written and yet hazy—typical of Washington, a master of ambiguity who upon command could turn a baffling phrase. For decades the letter's absence was proof for many that it was a forgery. Even the great historian Douglas Southall Freeman, who learned to know Washington well over the years that it took him to write his seven-volume biography of Washington, declared the letter a fake. But when the letter came on the manuscript market in the late twentieth century its authenticity could no longer be disputed. It is in Washington's strong hand, and the context fits with his other correspondence of the period.

50 So what is so unusual about the letter to Sally?

To begin with, it is a love letter, and not many from Washington have survived. Washington declares himself "a Votary of love," and says that he is in love with a lady. What frustrates readers is that he seems to be confessing his love to Sally. He then insists that the "world has no business to know the object of my Love, declared in this manner to you, when I want to conceal it." What is perturbing is that Washington had recently become engaged to the widow Martha Custis, who he also mentions in the letter. Hence the disagreements about the object of Washington's love—Sally, Martha, or a third lady, possibly Mary Cary, the sister of Sally who had revived Washington's spirits when he was trying to assuage the pain of not winning the "Low Land Beauty" several years earlier.

> 'Tis true, I profess myself a votary of love. I acknowledge that a lady is in the case, and further I confess that this lady is known to you. Yes, Madame, as well as she is to one who is too sensible of her charms to deny the Power whose influence he feels and must ever submit to. I feel the force of her amiable beauties in the recollection of a thousand tender passages that I could wish to obliterate, till I am bid to revive them.
> —George Washington to Sally Fairfax, 1758

A second letter to Sally, written two weeks after the first but never in dispute, was seen in a new light after the appearance of the "Votary of love" missive. Sally had replied to Washington that she had not fully understood his meanings. Her letter has never surfaced, but from Washington's reply it is clear that she also had referred to Joseph Addison's play, *Cato: A Tragedy*, herself playing the part of Marcia, the daughter of Cato, who sends away her secret lover Juba to war. Washington's reply contained a statement seemingly more direct than anything he said in the first letter: "I should think my time more agreeable spent believe me, in playing a part in Cato, with the Company you mention, and myself doubly happy in being he Juba to such a Marcia, as you must make." Without doubt that statement is flirtatious. But whether its intent is playful or serious (barring further evidence) will always be open to interpretation.

And there the matter rests for us, whether there was smoke, fire, or only a puff.

> *Do we still misunderstand the true meaning of each other's Letters? I think it must appear so, tho' I would feign hope the contrary as I cannot speak plainer without, But I'll say no more, and leave you to guess the rest.*
> —George Washington to Sally Fairfax, 1758

51 Did Washington's friendship continue with Sally and George William Fairfax?

Yes, very much so. Both families frequently visited one another's homes until George William and Sally Fairfax left for England in 1773. When they departed they invested in Washington power of attorney over all their business affairs in America, including the Belvoir estate. In describing the dilapidation of Belvoir in 1785, Washington told the Fairfaxes that "the happiest moments of my life had been spent there," and his pathetic description left Sally with "many tears & sighs." In 1798 Washington still lamented the passing of Belvoir, as though it symbolized the passing of his own life, "the ruins can only be viewed as the memento of former pleasures."

52 Did Washington love Martha?

Undoubtedly. Contemporaries noted that George and Martha had what we today would call a good marriage, an affectionate relationship filled with mutual respect and dependence. By all accounts their home life was marred only by the deaths of their children Patsy in 1773 and her older brother Jacky eight years later, and other family members and in-laws. As he informed a French correspondent who had recently tied the knot, "In my estimation more permanent and genuine happiness is to be found in the sequestered walks of connubial life, than in the giddy rounds of promiscuous pleasure, or the more tumultuous and imposing scenes of successful ambition." A surviving note from Washington to his wife, written at the end of a letter from Washington to a male correspondent at Mount Vernon, begins affectionately with the words, "My Love."

53 So Washington was Martha's second husband?

Yes, Martha married Daniel Parke Custis in June 1749, about five months before his father John Custis died leaving Daniel heir to one of the wealthiest estates in the Virginia colony. Martha gave birth to four children, all with the middle name of Parke—Daniel, Frances, Martha ("Patsy"), and John ("Jacky")—before her husband died in July 1757. Martha and George Washington married on 6 January 1759, only eighteen months after her first husband's death. The newlyweds settled at Mount Vernon with Martha's two youngest children, Patsy and Jacky, the older two children having died young, before the death of their father.

54   Was it a marriage for convenience sake?

Well, it did not hurt that both George and Martha had valuable assets to bring to their marriage. Martha was richer for sure (or at least her minor son Jacky was), having several plantations, a large number of slaves, and—a rarity in colonial Virginia—actual silver currency. Washington by surveying in the Fairfax Proprietary had added several thousand acres of land to his inheritances, Mount Vernon and Ferry Farm. He too owned a number of slaves, and was owed land by the British government for his French and Indian War service. Thus the marriage benefited both: Washington gained control of one of the wealthiest estates in Virginia, and Martha found a capable administrator.

55   Where did the wedding take place?

Although contemporary evidence is lacking, family lore says George and Martha's wedding ceremony took place at Martha's home, a Custis plantation on the Pamunkey River in New Kent County, Virginia, called the White House. Confederate General Robert E. Lee, who married Martha's great-granddaughter Mary Anna Randolph Custis, wrote that the ceremony took place in the parlor of the house, and was conducted by Reverend David Mossom. Another writer in the nineteenth century claimed that the ceremony took place in nearby St. Peter's Church.

The White House plantation passed from Martha's first husband to their son Jacky Custis, then to his son George Washington Parke Custis, and finally to William Henry Fitzhugh ("Rooney") Lee, the second son of Robert E. Lee. The Federal army occupied the plantation during the 1862 Peninsula Campaign and burned the house when it retreated during the Seven Days Battles.

56 What did Martha do during the Revolutionary War?

Believe it or not, she often accompanied General George in the field! In the eighteenth century, war tended to be conducted by seasonal campaigns, meaning that there were long periods of time when it was unlikely that the opposing armies would meet. During those times Martha traveled from Virginia to the Continental army headquarters, and stayed with her husband. The purpose of Martha's visits, wrote her friend Mercy Otis Warren, was "to soften the hours of private life, to sweeten the cares of a hero, and smooth the rugged paths of war." While with the army, conscious of her example as the wife of the commander in chief, Martha took part in the war effort by rallying other women to make or gather supplies for Continental troops.

When Martha was in Virginia her husband typically brooded about her "lonesome Situation," and relied on her brother-in-law Burwell Bassett to carry her and her son Jacky to his estate, Eltham, so she could be with family. Likewise, concern for Martha's feelings caused Washington to have Jacky surreptitiously inoculated against smallpox.

> *I learn from the Virginia officers that Mrs. Washington has ever been honored as a lady of distinguished goodness, possessing all the virtues which adorn her sex, amiable in her temper and deportment, full of benignity, benevolence, and charity, seeking for objects of affliction and poverty, that she may extend to the sufferer the hand of kindness and relief. These surely are the attributes which reveal a heart replete with those virtues which are so appropriate and estimable in the female character.*
> —James Thatcher, Journal entry, 1779

57 Did Martha make a good First Lady?

Yes! Lady Washington was the *first* First Lady, and like her husband conscious of her precedent-setting example before the public. She accepted her husband's call to more public service with as much grace, determination, and cheerfulness as she could, although she was reluctant to abandon the "endearing society" of family and friends at Mount Vernon. While in New York and Philadelphia she managed the presidential households and entertained guests, which included hosting ceremonial receptions at the presidential mansions. In that context Washington's secretary Tobias Lear described her as "one of those superior beings who are sent down to bless good men." She called the presidential period her "lost years."

> *I am now I beleive fixd at this Seat with an agreable Consort for Life and hope to find more happiness in retirement than I ever experienc'd amidst a wide and bustling World.*
>
> —George Washington to Richard Washington, 1759

58 Was Washington childless?

Yes and no. It is true that he fathered no children. But he raised children and grandchildren. Martha brought her two youngest children to their marriage, the elder two having died young. Martha Parke ("Patsy") Custis died of epilepsy in 1773 and John Parke ("Jacky") Custis of camp fever at Yorktown in 1781. Jacky was the only one of Martha's children to live long enough to marry and have children of his own, and after his sudden death his widow sent their two youngest children to Mount Vernon to live with their grandparents. Together, then, Martha and George raised four children. Moreover, they took an active role in the education of several nieces and nephews.

All in all, George and Martha were indulgent parents who spoiled their children. Their grandson especially, called variously Wash and

Tub, was the pet of the family. Like his father Jacky, Wash was able to resist all of Washington's efforts to see him properly educated. Washington's fruitless attempt to bend his boys' minds toward their studies is humorously chronicled in Washington's correspondence.

> *From his [George Washington Parke Custis's] infancy, I have discovered an almost unconquerable disposition to indolence in every thing that did not tend to his amusements: and have exhorted him in the most parental and friendly manner, often, to devote his time to more useful pursuits. His pride has been stimulated, and his family expectation & wishes have been urged, as inducements thereto. In short, I could say nothing to him now, by way of admonition—encouragement—or advice, that has not been repeated over & over again.*
> —George Washington to
> Samuel Stanhope Smith, 1797

59 Was Washington sterile?

Possibly, since Martha had four children by her first husband. Speculation on possible causes has ranged from genetic abnormalities to congenital causes to sexual dysfunction to mercury poisoning to complications from known or undiagnosed diseases, including tuberculosis and sexually transmitted diseases.

On the other hand, Martha thought that she was at fault, that her pregnancy with Patsy had brought on complications that prevented future conceptions, or that her bout with measles had made her infertile. George held out the hope that she would conceive until it was obvious that age had reckoned it impossible.

At age fifty-four Washington wrote that if Martha should survive him "there is a moral certainty of my dying without issue, and should I be the longest liver, the matter in my opinion is almost as certain; for whilst I retain the reasoning faculties I shall never marry a girl; and it is not probable that I should have children by a woman of an age suitable to my own, should I be disposed to enter into a second marriage."

Whatever the cause, Washington wanted to father an heir, and it was one of the greatest sorrows of his life that he did not do so.

> *It will be recollected, that the Divine Providence hath not seen fit, that my blood should be transmitted or my name perpetuated by the endearing, though sometimes seducing channel of immediate offspring. I have no child for whom I could wish to make a provision—no family to build in greatness upon my Country's ruins.*
> —George Washington, discarded draft of his
> First Inaugural Address, 1789

60 Did Washington father children by a slave woman?

Not likely. (Impossible if he was sterile.) Some have contended that Washington had a secret liaison with a slave woman named Venus, who lived at Bushfield, the plantation of his brother John Augustine Washington. (Washington was an infrequent visitor to Bushfield, some ninety-five miles away.) Venus did have a mulatto son, West Ford, who was set free by the terms of the Last Will and Testament of John Augustine's wife, Hannah Bushrod Washington. Hannah's son, Supreme Court Justice Bushrod Washington, who was George Washington's nephew and heir, brought Ford and other Bushfield house slaves to Mount Vernon when he moved there in 1802 after the death of Martha Washington. Ford became prominent in the Fairfax County free black community and lived in the vicinity until his death in 1863.

61 What did Washington think of slavery?

Washington was born into a society whose economic foundation relied heavily on slave labor. Only eleven years old when his father died and left him about a dozen slaves, Washington seemed to embrace the system uncritically, for he occasionally added to that number when he came of age. When he married Martha he gained control of the Custis slaves, a labor force significantly larger than his own, although he never would own any of these outright because they passed on to Martha's children and grandchildren. Intermarriage between the two groups of bondsmen eventually created unsolvable problems for Washington.

Over time, Washington began to think that the country would be better off without slavery. Like many in Virginia, he regarded the slave trade as "wicked cruel and unnatural," a "great inhumanity." His own labor needs changed when he abandoned the labor-intensive tobacco crop for wheat, which required many fewer hands. That created additional problems in that Washington was keen to keep families intact. In his eyes slaves were untrustworthy and could not be left idle. Moreover, in his opinion slavery as a labor system was inefficient and he perceived that the system was in decline in the northern colonies—yet those colonies continued to prosper.

As Washington grew older the ethical and moral considerations began to bear on him, and when he became the first person on the continent his thoughts of his own example began to weigh heavily on his mind. The subject began to creep into his letters. He confided to his farm manager and kinsman Lund Washington that "to be plain I wish to get quit of Negroes." To another he asserted his intention to never purchase another slave. To several correspondents he expressed his wish to see the legislature abolish the system by "slow, sure & imperceptible degrees." He possessed this "certain species of property," he declared, "very repugnantly to my own feelings." Given the circumstances of his finances, however, he felt powerless to extricate himself from the system.

> *With respect to the other species of property, concerning which you ask my opinion, I shall frankly declare to you that I do not like even to think much less talk of it. However, as you have put the question, I shall, in a few words, give you my ideas of it. Were it not then, that I am principled agt selling Negroes, as you would Cattle in the market, I would not, in twelve months from this date, be possessed of one as a slave.*
>
> —George Washington to
> Alexander Spotswood, 1794

62 Did Washington free any slaves?

Yes, in his Last Will and Testament. Washington expected the issue of slavery to eventually overwhelm the entire country and possibly disrupt the union. In that he proved prophetic, and although he did not feel that he could set free his slaves immediately while alive, he apparently wanted to be on the "right" side of history. Thus Washington made extensive provisions in his will concerning his slaves.

In effect, all the slaves owned outright by Washington would be set free upon the death of Martha. In addition to being set free, provisions were made for assisting the young, old, and infirm; for teaching reading and writing; for training in a useful occupation; and for preventing their being sold or transported out of Virginia "under any pretence whatsoever." These provisions were faithfully executed.

> *And I do moreover most pointedly, and most solemnly enjoin it upon my Executors . . . to see that this clause respecting Slaves, and every part thereof be religiously fulfilled at the Epoch at which it is directed to take place; without evasion, neglect or delay.*
> —George Washington,
> Last Will and Testament, 1799

63 What about Billy Lee?

William ("Billy") Lee was the most famous slave in eighteenth-century America. Washington purchased Billy from Mary Smith Ball Lee, then a two-time widow from Westmoreland County whose first husband was a cousin once removed of Washington's mother, Mary Ball. Billy was at the time, May 1768, a teenager, for whom Washington paid £61.15. For many years Billy was a fixture at Washington's side, serving with his master throughout the Revolutionary War. During the war Billy married a Margaret Thomas, a free black who worked in Washington's military family. Margaret apparently never visited

Mount Vernon even though Washington tried to arrange her passage from Philadelphia.

Billy fell and broke his knee while surveying with Washington in 1785, and thereafter was partly lame. Three years later he fell again and broke the other knee, and was forced to cease serving as Washington's valet and butler. Billy then took up cobbling shoes at Mount Vernon, where he remained the rest of his life. In Washington's will Lee was given the choice of immediate freedom or to remain at Mount Vernon, with an annuity of thirty dollars in either case.

> *He has been an old & faithful Servt. This is enough*
> *for the Presidt to gratify him in every reasonable wish.*
> —Tobias Lear to Clement Biddle, 1784

64 What was Washington's religious faith?

Washington was a lifelong member of the Anglican Church in Virginia, in which he was baptized, married, and served as a godfather for the children of several relatives and friends. He was a member of the Truro Parish Vestry from 1763 to 1784, but he ceased to take an active part after 1774 because of his prolonged absence from Mount Vernon. He served as a churchwarden three times. During his presidency Washington attended St. Paul's Chapel and Trinity Church in New York City and Christ Church and St. Peter's in Philadelphia. Washington's attitudes toward religion and his habits of church attendance did not change much over the course of his life.

65 Why have people questioned Washington's orthodoxy on religious matters?

For several reasons. First, Washington was not always a frequent attendee to religious services. He seems to have hardly noticed the Great Awakening that swept through the colonies while he was a child and a young man. He did not take communion, although Martha was a "habitual communicant." Nor did he seem to delight in reading religious sermons and pamphlets, like Martha.

Most damning, say those who consider Washington unorthodox in religious matters, is that he rarely mentioned the tenants of Christianity, the person of Jesus, or the afterlife in language typical of Christians. Rather, he usually referred to God as "Providence" or "Heaven." His terms for the deity are remote: the "Higher Cause," the "Great Ruler of Events," the "Supreme Ruler," the "Supreme Architect of the Universe," the "Governor of the Universe," the "Director of Human Events," the "Author of the Universe," the "Author of all good," the "beneficent Being," the "Sovereign Dispenser of life and health," the "Great Creator," and etc. These terms seem to describe the aloof God of Deism, which was in vogue in the eighteenth century.

66 Then was Washington a Deist?

Some think so but others hotly contest this view. Clearly Washington used the language prevalent in Deism, and his seeming lack of enthusiasm about religious matters have led some to think he was at least a "passive" Deist. But many others at the time, including orthodox Christian ministers, used the same language. Washington seems not to have thought about religion in philosophical terms, and his personal religious practices took place in the context of Episcopalism.

A persuasive case has been made that Washington fit squarely in the Latitudinarian stream of eighteenth-century episcopalism that dominated the Church of England and the Episcopal Church in America. Latitudinarians conformed to official Anglican practices but felt that matters of doctrine, organization, and observance are ultimately of little consequence and hence beliefs about them are more or less a matter of one's personal preference. This explains Washington's broadmindedness and tolerance in religious matters.

67 Then what were Washington's religious beliefs?

It is extremely difficult to tease out Washington's personal religious convictions—he kept those to himself. A search of his writings finds him quite elusive on the subject. He formed his religious vocabulary after his usual fashion of borrowing, using, and discarding phrases of language from others as the occasion arose. He typically did not write about religion per se although he often referred to Providence's role in protecting America during the Revolution and establishing the national government. Although Washington's religious behavior can be discovered with some sense of certainty, the principles governing those practices remain obscure.

A few things can be said, if we rely on Washington's terminology. Washington believed that the "ways of Providence," manifested through "invisible workings," are just and kind and wise but are ultimately "inscrutable." Humans, too small to comprehend these acts, nevertheless should recognize and stand in awe of them. One can even hope that Providence might decree otherwise than what seems apparent. And Providence intervenes in the affairs of individuals, peoples, and nations. Although life's outcomes are uncertain, divine favor must be sought; and faith and gratitude are indispensable. Some acts of Providence are irreversible and must be acquiesced to—death is the prime example. Yet the sting of death is tempered by thoughts of a "happier clime," the "land of Spirits"—although Washington declined to define his conception of an afterlife. Finally, Washington believed that religion serves an important civic purpose, underpinning morality, toleration, and liberty of conscience.

> *The hand of Providence has been so conspicuous in all this, that he must be worse than an infidel that lacks faith, and more than wicked, that has not gratitude enough to acknowledge his obligations, but, it will be time enough for me to turn preacher, when my present appointment ceases; and therefore, I shall add no more on the Doctrine of Providence.*
> —George Washington to Thomas Nelson, 1778

The ways of Providence being inscrutable, and the justice of it not to be scanned by the shallow eye of humanity, not to be counteracted by the utmost efforts of human power or wisdom, resignation, and as far as the strength of our reason and religion can carry us, a cheerful acquiescence to the Divine Will, is what we are to aim.

—George Washington to Burwell Bassett, 1773

My first remaining wish being, to glide gently down the stream of life in tranquil retirement till I shall arrive at the world of Sperits.

—George Washington to Robert Morris, 1787

68 What about the role of religion in the public sphere?

Washington supported chaplains in the army during both the French and Indian and the Revolutionary Wars. Observance of the Sabbath, appeals to Providence, and days set aside for thanksgiving were commonplace. He believed that Providence had a direct hand in bringing about the American Revolution. When he became president, Washington made it a point to answer all the appeals and wishes of good will that were sent to him from religious assemblies across the country. Washington also had no problem with the public support of religion by taxation—Episcopalians support their churches, Baptists support theirs, Jews support their synagogues, etc. In his First Inaugural Address Washington went out of his way not to omit his "fervent supplications" to the "Almighty Being who rules over the Universe" and stressed the role of Providence in establishing the United States. To Washington, organized religion was indispensable to morality, a pillar of the social order, a theme elaborated in his Farewell Address.

No People can be bound to acknowledge and adore the invisible hand, which conducts the Affairs of men more than the People of the United States.

—George Washington,
First Inaugural Address, 1789

Reason & experience both forbid us to expect that
National morality can prevail in exclusion of religious
principle.
    —George Washington, Farewell Address, 1796

69 So Washington mentions religion in his Farewell Address?

Yes. In fact, the Farewell Address contains Washington's clearest and most public statement on the relationship between religion and society. For Washington, religion and morality are necessary for human happiness and main props of civilized society, and politicians would do well to respect them. His statements contained in the Farewell Address are eloquent but like references to religion in many of his other writings he declined to define what he meant by the terms, leaving that for his readers.

Of all the dispositions and habits which lead to political
prosperity, Religion and morality are indispensable
supports. In vain would that man claim the tribute of
Patriotism, who should labour to subvert these great
Pillars of human happiness, these firmest props of the duties
of Men & citizens. The mere Politician, equally with the
pious man ought to respect & to cherish them. A volume
could not trace all their connections with private & public
felicity. Let it simply be asked where is the security for
property, for reputation, for life, if the sense of religious
obligation desert the Oaths, which are the instruments of
investigation in Courts of Justice? And let us with caution
indulge the supposition, that morality can be maintained
without religion.
    —George Washington, Farewell Address, 1796

70 Religious tolerance?

Washington was ahead of his time in matters of religious tolerance. Partly his attitude arose from the Latitudinarian principles of his church, but no doubt he also was informed by his extensive travels up and down the eastern seaboard and into the backcountry, where he saw the diversity of the American people. By the time of his presidency he could wish "every temporal and spiritual felicity" to Baptists, Quakers, Catholics, and Jews alike. To the latter Washington wrote that the new United States government gave "to bigotry no sanction, to persecution no assistance."

71 What is Washington's Prayer?

This widely circulated but misleading document is actually part of the text of a circular address to the governors of the thirteen states that Washington wrote near the end of the Revolutionary War. The phrases "Almighty God" and "Through Jesus Christ Our Lord" are placed at the beginning and end of the so-called prayer, but do not appear on any of the original copies sent to the governors. A paragraph of the circular, however, does express a strong religious sentiment.

72 What is the Washington Prayer Journal?

A collection of Washington family relics sold in 1891 included a pocket memorandum book containing twenty-four handwritten pages of prayers based on the Book of Common Prayer. A manuscript dealer offered it for sale as a manuscript supposedly written by George Washington when he was about twenty years old. The Smithsonian Institute already had rejected the manuscript as inauthentic, and others subsequently challenged its authenticity as well. Nevertheless the "The Daily Sacrifice," as it was titled, began to circulate as "Washington's Prayers," Washington's Prayer Book," and "Washington's Prayer Journal." The manuscript is not in Washington's writing, however, as easy comparison with the many thousands of genuine documents in Washington's writing makes clear.

73 Did Washington really pray in the snow at Valley Forge?

Chalk up another one to Parson Weems. Originally appearing in the seventeenth edition of the cleric's wildly popular Life of Washington (Philadelphia, 1817), this story, perhaps more than any other, helped convince nineteenth-century America that Washington had been a man of deep Christian piety. If the picturesque scene of Washington on his knees in the snow pleading with God for the sake of his troops was not enough to make a believer out of those who encountered the story, then the supposed conversion of a peace-loving Quaker into a supporter of the American war effort tended to lend extra credibility.

In the winter of '77, while Washington, with the American army lay encamped at Valley Forge, a certain good old FRIEND, of the respectable family and name of Potts, if I mistake not, had occasion to pass through the woods near head-quarters. Treading his way along the venerable grove, suddenly he heard the sound of a human voice, which as he advanced increased on his ear, and at length became like the voice of one speaking much in earnest. As he approached the spot with a cautious step, whom should he behold, in a dark natural bower of ancient oaks, but the commander in chief of the American armies on his knees at prayer! Motionless with surprise, friend Potts continued on the place till the general, having ended his devotions, arose, and, with a countenance of angel serenity, retired to headquarters: friend Potts then went home, and on entering his parlour called out to his wife, "Sarah, my dear! Sarah! All's well! all's well! George Washington will yet prevail!"
—Mason Locke Weems, *Life of Washington*, 1817

It was a bad winter at Valley Forge, and no wonder Washington might have been caught in the act of pleading with the Almighty to provide for his army. Although Quaker Isaac Potts owned the house that served as Washington's headquarters at Valley Forge, he lived elsewhere at the time. Potts's aunt, Deborah Pyewell Potts Hewes, the widow of Thomas Potts II and the wife of Caleb Hewes, occupied the house. Moreover, a second version of the story—appearing after Weems's—supposedly a first-hand account related by Potts himself, gives the name of the observer as John Potts, Isaac's brother, an iron monger who also was not at Valley Forge that winter.

74 What about the influence of Stoicism?

Washington seems to have liberally absorbed the basic tenets of Stoic philosophy as a youth. (The Fairfax family at Belvoir, which gave Washington his start, is said to have been attracted to the philosophy.) With its emphasis on courage, justice, wisdom, temperance, and acceptance of the divine will, Stoicism appealed to Washington as it did to early Christians and Deists alike. Washington's conscious embracement of Stoicism influenced his religious and philosophical opinions and served him well when he was in the throes of his last illness and death.

75 Was Washington a Freemason?

Yes, Washington was initiated as an apprentice in the Masonic Lodge of Fredericksburg, Virginia, in November 1752. In March 1753 he "pass'd fellow Craft" and the following August became a Master Mason. Freemasonry was popular in eighteenth-century Virginia, and for the young Washington his initiation into the secret and mysterious rites of the fraternity signified his formal entry into genteel society. Initiates acknowledged their belief in God and the immortality of the soul and pledged themselves to Freemasonry's "true principles": fraternity, universal love, morality, acts of benevolence, and loyalty to civic laws and values.

Freemasonry entered America the year Washington was born, and to him it represented just the kind of social organization needed to school the new republic in moral virtue. The "grand object of Masonry," he declared, "is to promote the happiness of the human race." His affiliation has been thorny to both Masons and non-Masons alike, however. Members proudly point to his ties to the fraternity and how he symbolizes its ideals of honor, honesty, and religious tolerance. Others cynically note that Washington's commitment to the fraternity was by his own admission nominal, that he rarely attended meetings, and that his letters mention the subject only in reply to others who had broached it first.

Even if Washington did not frequent lodge meetings he willingly took part in funerals and celebrations where Masons played an active part. The most famous was the ceremonial laying of the cornerstone of the United States Capitol in September 1793, in which Washington appeared in full Masonic regalia. Masons officially participated in Washington's funeral as well, performing their rites, although Washington had left instructions for a private burial. Many lodges bestowed honorary membership upon Washington after he became famous.

> *I request you will be assured of my best wishes and earnest prayers for your happiness while you remain in this terrestrial Mansion, and that we may hereafter meet as brethren in the Eternal Temple of the Supreme Architect.*
>
> —George Washington to
> the Grand Lodge of Pennsylvania, 1792

76 Was Washington also a member of the Illuminati?

No. The Order of the Illuminati was a secret society within Freemasonry founded in 1776 by a group of freethinkers in Bavaria who embraced the more progressive ideals of the Enlightenment. The order opposed political and religious authority as unnatural and unreasonable and sought to remake society not through political revolution but by bringing enlightening perfection to mankind. Eventually the movement numbered about three thousand adherents in some half dozen European countries, but it never made inroads in America. Washington had heard of the Illuminati by 1798 when a correspondent sent him a copy of John Robison's polemic against Illuminism and Jacobinism, *Proofs of a Conspiracy Against All Religions and Governments of Europe* (London, 1798). When thanking the sender for the book Washington declared that none of the lodges of Freemasons in America had been contaminated with the principles ascribed to the Illuminati.

Despite Washington's assertions that he was only a nominal Freemason and that he knew nothing of the Illuminati, some modern-day conspiracy theorists continue to claim that Washington was part of a worldwide movement whose master plan was (and is) to overthrow rulers and governments and run the world through a secret shadow government.

I have heard much of the nefarious, and dangerous plan, and doctrines of the Illuminati, but never saw the Book until you were pleased to send it to me. The same causes which have prevented my acknowledging the receipt of your letter have prevented my reading the Book, hitherto; namely, the multiplicity of matters which pressed upon me before, and the debilitated state in which I was left after, a severe fever had been removed. And which allows me to add little more now, than thanks for your kind wishes and favourable sentiments, except to correct an error you have run into, of my Presiding over the English lodges in this Country. The fact is, I preside over none, nor have I been in one more than once or twice, within the last thirty years. I believe notwithstanding, that none of the Lodges in this Country are contaminated with the principles ascribed to the Society of the Illuminati.

—George Washington to
George Washington Snyder, 1798.

61

77 Did Washington have any close friends?

Yes, some for a lifetime. He was especially close to people around him, and then some others, including a number of Virginians. Those included Dr. James Craik, his physician and colleague during both the French and Indian and the Revolutionary Wars, probably his closest friend. David Stuart, also a physician and the husband of the widow of Martha Washington's son John Parke Custis was another close friend. He was also very close to Fielding Lewis (the husband of his sister Betty), and Burwell Bassett, Martha's brother-in-law. In later years Washington was close to grandson George Washington Parke Custis and nephew Bushrod Washington, to whom he left Mount Vernon, as well as his secretary Tobias Lear, who married in succession two of Martha's nieces. Richard Henry Lee was a life-long friend, and neighbor George Mason was a close colleague although the exact nature of their friendship is uncertain.

During the Revolutionary War Washington made a host of new friends, many younger than himself: Joseph Reed, the marquis de Lafayette, Alexander Hamilton, and John Laurens, as well as Philip Schuyler, Nathanael Greene, Henry Laurens, and Henry ("Light-Horse Harry") Lee. Benedict Arnold was a favorite but his treason of course turned Washington against him.

And there were women among those that can be counted as close to Washington: His wife Martha ranks number one, of course, but also his sister Betty Lewis, his granddaughter Nelly Custis, and Sally Fairfax.

78 Did Washington ever travel abroad?

No, the farthest that Washington traveled was to the West Indies. As a young man he accompanied his half brother Lawrence to Barbados during the winter of 1751–1752. Lawrence went to the Leeward Islands in search of restorative cures for his rapidly failing health—the quest proved fruitless. While in Barbados George became infected with a mild case of smallpox that lasted about a month and that immunized him against the disease.

After the Revolutionary War Washington did think about traveling to Europe, and even made very preliminary plans to do so, but abandoned the idea as unrealistic.

79 How about travels on the American continent?

Washington visited all thirteen colonies. In fact, he was one of the most traveled persons in America. As a young surveyor he traversed the Virginia backcountry, up and down the Shenandoah Valley, at that time America's western frontier. During the French and Indian War his missions took him to the Ohio Country, to the area of present-day Pittsburgh, Pennsylvania, and to Boston. He spent the Revolutionary War years living in Massachusetts, New York, New Jersey, Pennsylvania, and other places. In his first presidential administration he made tours that took in all thirteen states, first to New England in 1789, and then South in 1791. Through these extensive travels Washington was able to see first-hand the differences and similarities of life across the land.

80 Did Washington ever fight a duel?

No, Washington detested the practice of dueling. He personally never entered into a duel, and he outlawed the practice in the Continental army, placing it in the category of serious crimes that also included mutiny, treason, plundering, and sleeping on guard duty. Ironically, several of Washington's army officers fought duels, as did at least two of his aides-de-camp, John Laurens (in 1778), and Alexander Hamilton (after Washington's death). Another duel took place in the aftermath of the Conway Cabal, the attempt to have Washington removed from the head of the army.

81 Was Washington in the Virginia militia?

No. Washington's first military appointment was made in January 1754 when Virginia Governor Robert Dinwiddie commissioned him captain of one of two one-hundred-men companies being raised to guard the Ohio Company's laborers at the Forks of the Ohio, the point where the Allegheny and Monongahela Rivers converge to form the Ohio River.

Only two weeks later the Virginia House of Burgesses resolved to expand the expedition and authorized the establishment of the Virginia Regiment, a special provincial force to consist of three hundred volunteers. Washington was named its lieutenant colonel. Neither of his commissions was granted as part of the militia system. In August 1755, after the colonel of the Virginia Regiment, Joshua Fry, was killed in a riding accident, Washington was promoted to colonel. Washington served as colonel of the Virginia Regiment, through subsequent reorganizations, until late 1758.

82 Did Washington seek a British army commission?

Yes, but he did not get it. The two role models of his youth, half brother Lawrence and neighbor William Fairfax, both held British commissions and were veterans of wars. Their examples coupled with Washington's aspirations and sense of adventure made the military life appealing. In 1754, when he was but twenty-two years old, he succinctly summed up his military ambitions: "My inclinations are strongly bent to arms."

Over the next three years, as an officer in Virginia's provincial forces, Washington consciously emulated his regular British army counterparts, hoping to prove himself worthy of a royal commission. And he succeeded, so much so that he won the admiration of professional British officers. Yet the coveted commission failed to materialize, even after direct personal appeals to British Generals Braddock, Shirley, and Loudoun. Governor Dinwiddie and the Virginia House of Burgesses also actively petitioned for Washington and his subordinate officers to be granted regular army commissions, even on a temporary basis, as had been the case with provincial officers in some of the other colonies, but those appeals also fell on deaf ears. In the end, Washington abandoned his efforts to acquire a British army commission.

Interestingly, Washington did not try to purchase a commission, an option made use of by many in the period. Apparently, it was a matter of honor to him that his own merits and those of the officers in his regiment receive from the British authorities the recognition that he felt they deserved.

83 What was the Dagworthy Controversy?

It was a disagreement in the fall of 1755 about military rank between Washington and John Dagworthy, a native of New Jersey then living in Maryland. Dagworthy claimed that his royal commission as captain, granted in 1746 during the British-American expedition against the French in Canada, gave him precedence over all colonial officers at Fort Cumberland, Maryland, where the Virginia Regiment was posted. Washington, who held a provincial commission as colonel, resisted Dagworthy's assertion but avoided a direct challenge by staying away from Fort Cumberland and his regiment. When informed of the matter, Governor Dinwiddie sided with Washington.

Dinwiddie gave Washington leave to travel to Boston to ask the commander of all the British forces in America, General William Shirley, to settle the issue. Shirley's assessment of the situation was that Dagworthy's royal commission expired in 1747 when the expedition to Canada was abandoned and that Dagworthy presently served as a provincial captain. Dagworthy was thus to be under Washington's command when in service together. Dagworthy submitted to Shirley's decree and the controversy ended, although when the Virginia Regiment left Fort Cumberland in 1757 Dagworthy resumed command.

The Dagworthy Controversy revealed Washington's sensitivity to issues of deference and rank. It gave him his first opportunity to travel to New England, and also introduced him to the commander in chief of all the British forces in America.

84 Did Washington start the French and Indian War?

Yes, but he really did not mean to. And he had some help from Virginia Governor Robert Dinwiddie.

The background to the start of hostilities lay in an unusual proposal that Washington made to Dinwiddie in the fall of 1753. He would, Washington told the governor, "go properly commissioned to the Commandant of the French Forces, to learn by what Authority he presumes to make Incroachments on his Majesty's Lands on the Ohio." At twenty-one years of age, with no military experience, Washington was showing the audacity that came to characterize his military career.

What was just as audacious, is that Dinwiddie, also with no military experience but in charge of the military affairs of Virginia—and with an order from the Crown to drive off by force of arms anyone encroaching on British settlements—accepted Washington's offer. Dinwiddie, with no military advisors, not even a British army officer in the colony, badly wanted to learn about the Ohio Country. The governor had learned that the French were making incursions into the region and that hostile Indians were harassing frontier British settlements, but until Washington made his proposition, Dinwiddie had no chance to act on the Crown's instructions to clear the frontier of intruders or to gain a better knowledge of frontier conditions.

Dinwiddie drafted a letter to the commandant of the French forces in the Ohio Country, Jacques Le Gardeur, sieur de Saint-Pierre, warning him to leave the region as it belonged to the British. Washington departed, accompanied by renowned frontier explorer Christopher Gist as guide and interpreter. And the mission was a success. He delivered the letter—which the commandant scoffed at—thereby seeing and sketching the formidable fort the French had constructed near the Ohio on French Creek, Fort Le Boeuf. He also made a map of the river systems of the Ohio Country. He met Indians, not only hostile ones but friendly ones who disliked the French. Washington kept a journal of his expedition, which Dinwiddie ordered printed upon Washington's return to Williamsburg—Washington became an instant celebrity—Dinwiddie charged him with another mission; this one led to bloodshed.

85 What was Washington's next role in the French and Indian War?

Now that Washington had started a war, Governor Dinwiddie decided to create a colonial force to protect the Ohio Company's workmen at the Forks of the Ohio. The Virginia Regiment, with Washington as lieutenant colonel, set out for the Ohio in early April. En route Washington discovered that the French had taken the Forks, so he redirected his troops to cut a new wagon road to a destination south of the Forks. Washington's expedition reached the Great Crossing of the Youghiogheny River in mid-May. Camping there until the 24th, Washington moved his men to Great Meadows, a "small marshy valley surrounded by sloping wooded hills."

Meanwhile, on 23 May, the French sent a party to meet the Virginians. Upon learning of the French approach from friendly Indians, Washington led his troops out in searching of the party. A short engagement ensued, and the French commander, Jumonville, was killed.

86 Did Washington assassinate Jumonville?

Well, it depends. Joseph Coulon de Villiers, sieur de Jumonville, the French army commandant at the unfinished French fortification at the Forks of the Ohio, Fort Duquesne, was on a mission with thirty-three men and an English interpreter to summon the Virginia troops to withdraw back across the mountains—a mission not unlike Washington's to the French the previous year. Warned by friendly Indians of the French approach, Washington formed his men "to attack them on all sides." During an engagement of fifteen minutes the Virginians took twenty-one prisoners and killed ten, including Jumonville, slain by "a Musket-Shot in the Head" or, depending on the source, tomahawked and scalped by Indians. It was Washington's first experience in battle, and he found it exhilarating.

Reports of the engagement were contradictory. Washington and his officers justified their actions on the basis that the French, with hostile intentions, had been stalking them for several days. The Indians wanted to kill the French captives but Washington sent them to Williamsburg. The French, on the other hand, claimed that they had been ambushed while attempting to deliver a peaceful message, and that the Indians had stopped the English from killing the prisoners.

The discrepancy in the accounts was underscored when Washington was defeated at Fort Necessity about five weeks later and signed articles of capitulation admitting that the Virginians had assassinated Jumonville. Washington and his fellow officers later claimed that the translation of the articles read to them made no mention of any assassination, and that if that had been their understanding they never would have signed the articles. Whatever had passed, the damage was done, for Washington's papers were confiscated and the articles of capitulation published in Europe.

87 So Washington found the heat of battle exhilarating?

Yes, if we are to believe Washington's own account of his first exposure to the hazards of combat. "I heard Bullets whistle," he declared, "and believe me there was something charming in the sound." The statement drew from King George II the comment that, "He would not say so, if he had been used to hear many." It might have been an immature quip, but it revealed the coolness that characterized Washington's battlefield demeanor.

> *I fortunately escaped without a wound, tho' the right Wing where I stood was exposed to & received all the Enemy's fire and was the part where the man was killed & the rest wounded. I can with truth assure you, I*

heard Bullets whistle and believe me there was something
charming in the sound.

—George Washington to
John Augustine Washington, 1754

88 So Washington was defeated at Fort Necessity?

Yes, in early July 1754. After the attack on Jumonville Washington
and his men fell back to their camp at Great Meadows, where they
hastily began building a temporary stockade, christened Fort Necessity.
When the fort was finished in early June, Washington declared it
capable of defending against an attack by five hundred French troops.
Provisions were low, however, and by the end of the month the French
had gathered a force of four hundred soldiers plus a contingent of
Indians under command of Louis Coulon de Villiers, Jumonville's
brother.

The combined force attacked Fort Necessity on 3 July in mid-
morning, and by 8:00 P.M., with a steady rain falling, Washington's
men were "without Shelter, in Trenches full of Water." The French
offered terms, and Washington accepted. Washington's troops, less
than four hundred, lost thirty killed and seventy wounded, while the
French had two killed and seventeen wounded. The ignominy of defeat
was compounded by the signing of the articles of capitulation in which
Washington unknowingly admitted assassinating Jumonville, and by
one final humiliation—the pilfering of the retreating troops' baggage
by Indians allied with the French. Washington's first campaign in war
he did not intend to start came to an inglorious end.

89 Did Washington take part in the Braddock Campaign?

Yes. After Washington's defeat at Fort Necessity the British
ministry sent two regular army regiments to America under the
command of Major General Edward Braddock, a seasoned officer
of the Coldstream Guards. He arrived in Virginia in February 1755,

followed by a thousand Irish troops. By early June, Braddock had gathered some 1,760 British and provincial troops in the vicinity of Wills Creek (the frontier headquarters of the Ohio Company in present-day Cumberland, Maryland), chosen as the advanced staging area for military operations against the French. Braddock planned to take Fort Duquesne from the French and rebuild it as a British garrison from which he would drive the French completely away from the Ohio country, the Great Lakes, and Nova Scotia.

Washington accompanied Braddock as a volunteer in his military family, hoping to form "an acquaintance which may be serviceable hereafter, if I can find it worth while to push my Fortune in the Military way." Although he answered to no one but Braddock, he communicated with Braddock through the general's chief aide-de-camp, Robert Orme, with whom he became quite friendly during the campaign.

> *The Gen'l. has appointed me one of his aids de Camps,*
> *in which Character I shall serve this Campaigne, agreeably*
> *enough, as I am thereby freed from all commands but his,*
> *and give Order's to all, which must be implicitly obey'd.*
> —George Washington to
> John Augustine Washington, 1755

Throughout June 1755 Braddock's army slowly made its way forward, with detachments of French and Indians harassing it along the way. About mid-June Washington fell sick with "Fevers and Pains" and after nearly a week of illness was compelled to fall to the rear as the army moved ahead. On the eve of the battle that took place on 9 July Washington was conveyed to the front in a covered wagon, and when the fighting commenced he offered to "head the Provincials, & engage the enemy in their own way; but the propriety of it was not seen into until it was too late for execution."

> *We have been most scandalously beaten by a trifling*
> *body of men.*
> —George Washington to
> John Augustine Washington, 1755

The battle lasted only two hours, but that was long enough for the British and provincials to suffer a complete rout, and the death of Braddock and many of his officers. (Of ninety-six officers, twenty-six were killed and thirty-six wounded.) Washington narrowly escaped becoming a casualty himself—one horse was killed and two wounded under him, a musket ball sliced through his hat, and several others through his clothes, but miraculously he made it through the day unharmed. Washington's emergence from Braddock's defeat unscathed led to the so-called Indian Prophecy that he would not die in battle.

> *When we came there, we were attackd by a body of French and Indns whose number (I am certain) did not exceed 300 Men; our's consisted of abt 1,300 well armed Troops;* chiefly *of the English Soldiers, who were struck with such a panick, that they behavd with more cowardice than it is possible to conceive.*
>
> —George Washington to
> Mary Ball Washington, 1755

Washington led the retreat, burying Braddock in the road along the way so that the general's grave could not be discovered. The troops regrouped at Great Meadows and from there retreated back into Maryland.

90 What was the Indian Prophecy?

The story that Washington would not die in battle was related by an old Indian chief who met Washington years later and declared that his warriors had tried to kill him but could not. Dr. James Craik, Washington's close friend and a comrade during the French and Indian War, told the story to George Washington Parke Custis, who adapted the account for the stage, in his *The Indian Prophecy, A National Drama, in Two Acts* (Washington, D.C., 1828). Custis also repeated the story in his *Recollections of Washington* (1859).

'Twas all in vain, a power mightier far than we, shielded him from harm. He can not die in battle. . . . Listen! The Great Spirit protects that man, and guides his destinies—he will become the chief of nations, and a people yet unborn will hail him as the founder of a mighty empire!

—George Washington Parke Custis,
A Memoir of the Indian Prophecy, 1828

91 Did Washington take part in the Forbes Campaign?

Yes, as colonel of the Virginia Regiment. After Braddock's defeat the British took three years to prepare a new campaign against the French at Fort Duquesne. John Forbes, colonel of the Seventeenth British Regiment and adjutant general on the staff of Lord Loudoun (Shirley's successor as commander in chief of the British forces in America), was given the additional rank of brigadier general for the operation. Forbes's forces consisted of eight thousand British and provincial troops, including the Virginia Regiment. Washington and his men were placed under the direct command of Lieutenant Colonel Henry Bouquet of the Royal American Regiment.

Washington attempted to persuade Forbes to take the route to the Ohio used three years earlier in the Braddock expedition, but Forbes would hear nothing of it, choosing instead to cut a fresh road through Pennsylvania. The new road, punctuated by a string of defensive posts, was cut quickly during the summer of 1758, and in September Forbes decided it was time to strike.

Forbes ordered his troops to march against Fort Duquesne, where according to Washington, "the enemy sallied out, and an obstinate Engagement began." Taken by surprise, the attackers were completely repulsed by a joint force of French and Indians. Washington's own command suffered heavy casualties; out of the one hundred and seventy-four members of the Virginia Regiment, sixty-two were killed. Following the humiliating encounter Forbes recuperated his army in Pennsylvania for two months before renewing the fight. The new stab gave rise to some light skirmishing before the French decided to burn Fort Duquesne and abandon the Ohio, effectively ending the French and Indian War.

> *The Enemy, after letting us get within a days march of the place, burned the fort, and ran away (by the light of it) at night, going down the Ohio by water, to the number of about 500 men, from our best information.*
> —George Washington to Francis Fauquier, 1758

92 Did Washington personally kill anyone in battle?

Nobody knows.

93 Why was Washington chosen commander in chief of the Continental army?

Because then, as now, military appointments were as much political as martial arrangements, and no one else in the colonies was as well positioned to garner the widespread support needed to satisfy the interests of all. Renowned for his French and Indian War service, eminent in the Continental Congress, and American born, he was acceptable to all the colonies—acceptable to Virginia, of course, but also agreeable to Massachusetts, where troops were already in the field facing the British.

94 Is it true that Washington accepted no pay as general?

Yes. When accepting Congress's appointment as commander in chief of the Continental army, Washington announced his intent of serving without compensation. Although he did not take a salary, he did accept reimbursement for the expenses related to maintaining his military family.

Such is his disinterested patriotism, that he assured Congress, on his appointment, that he should receive from the public, for his military services, no other compensation than the amount of his necessary expenses.
—James Thatcher, Journal entry, 1775

95 Was Washington a great general?

Yes. A general is not measured by the battles he has won, but by the leadership he provides. Lafayette illustrated this point, reminiscing late in his life about Washington's performance as a general. At the Battle of Monmouth, Lafayette recalled, "General Washington appeared to arrest fortune by one glance, and his presence of mind, valour, and decision of character, were never displayed to greater advantage than at that moment."

It is often exultingly remarked in our camp, that Washington was born for the salvation of his country, and that he is endowed with all, the talents and abilities necessary to qualify him for the great undertaking.
—James Thatcher, Journal entry, 1777

96 Did Washington lose all his battles and win the war?

Not really. Washington had some stunning successes as well as disappointing defeats. He also had some helpful and harmless draws. It is true that battlefield tactics was not Washington's forte, but the nature of eighteenth-century warfare was not such that battles were fought very frequently, and most battles were not of war-changing importance. By today's standards, many Revolutionary War battles were little more than skirmishes, but a triumph of any sort, large or small, was always welcome.

97 What was Washington's first Revolutionary War victory?

Forcing the British to leave Boston. The siege of Boston was already underway when Washington arrived at Cambridge to take command of the Continental army in July 1775. Hated by the local citizenry, poorly supplied, and generally demoralized, the British were as anxious to leave the province as the Americans were to see them go. The standoff lasted for another eight months, however, until the Americans finally fortified Dorchester Heights, the hills overlooking the city from across the Charles River, in March 1776.

The end of the siege was sudden and dramatic. Washington's troops threw up their fortifications overnight, surprising the British so completely that one eyewitness said the works were "raised with an expedition to equal to that of the Genii belonging to Aladdin's Wonderful Lamp." The British, wishing to avoid a recurrence of the bloody encounter at Bunker Hill, abandoned Boston after a few days of token opposition. Driving the British army out of Boston was a signal victory for Washington, and a boost to American morale.

> *The hills and elevations in this vicinity are covered with spectators to witness deeds of horror in the expected conflict. His Excellency General Washington is present, animating and encouraging the soldiers, and they in return manifest their joy, and express a warm desire for the approach of the enemy; each man knows his place, and is resolute to execute his duty.*
> —James Thatcher, Journal entry, 1776

98 How about Washington's first Revolutionary War defeat?

That took place on Long Island in August 1776. Washington had divided his army between Manhattan and Long Islands after following the British from Boston to New York in the spring and summer of 1776. Thinking New York City the British objective, Washington underestimated the size of the enemy forces on Long Island, which numbered about fifteen thousand. He therefore failed to adequately reinforce the real British objective, Brooklyn Heights, a strategic eminence dominating New York City. When Washington belatedly grasped the enemy's intentions he deployed an additional five thousand men, but by then he had been outflanked. British and Hessian troops, supported by five British warships, surprised and outnumbered Washington's forces, killing between two and three hundred men and capturing nearly another eleven hundred. British and Hessian casualties totaled about three hundred and fifty killed, wounded, and captured. Skirmishing between the opposing forces continued for a couple of days before Washington was able to save the remainder of his army by retreating back to Manhattan Island under the cover of a dense fog.

> *Having resolved to withdraw his army from its hazardous position, General Washington crossed over to the island in the night of the 29th of August, and personally conducted the retreat in so successful a manner, under the most embarrassing circumstances, that it is considered as a remarkable example of good generalship.*
> —James Thatcher, Journal entry, 1776

99 Did Washington make other major mistakes as commander in chief?

Oh yes—several! Kip's Bay, New York, in September 1776, was not a fine moment. Coming on the heels of the disastrous Battle of Long Island, the Americans were humiliated by the cannonade covering the British landing party at Kip's Bay, a tiny inlet on the east side of Manhattan Island. It was not so much that his men's courage failed—although that is the way it seemed to Washington and his aides-de-camp and even to the British, when his men "could not be brought to stand one shot." Rather, Washington had placed the wrong men—raw militia—in a position where too much was expected of them. Perhaps seasoned troops could have stood against the British regulars while a heavy cannonade scoured the ground around them, but these were not seasoned troops.

> *Sixty Light Infantry, upon the first fire, put to flight two brigades of the* Connecticut *troops—wretches who, however strange it may appear, from our Brigadier-General down to the private sentinel, were caned and whipped by the Generals* Washington, *[Israel]* Putnam, *and [Thomas]* Mifflin, *but even his indignity had no weight, they could not be brought to stand one shot.*
> —William Smallwood to
> the Maryland Convention, 1776

The Battle of White Plains in October and the capture of Forts Washington and Lee in November, followed by a hasty retreat across New Jersey to the Delaware River, added to what became a string of failures for Washington in 1776. White Plains might have been won had Washington fortified the high ground when he had a chance; at least his men proved once again that they could stand up against the regular British army, by inflicting twice the number of casualties than they received.

The loss of Fort Washington was more disastrous. Considered a critical component of the American defense system, Washington and Congress wanted to hold onto Fort Washington for as long as possible, as a base from which to harass British ships in the Hudson River. Unfortunately for Washington, he attempted to hold onto the fort after it became clear that the British would storm it, which led to the capture of twenty-nine hundred American prisoners and one hundred and fifty killed and wounded. On top of that, the British took forty-three pieces of artillery, a large supply of ammunition, and some of the best small arms in the possession of the Continental army. The costly defeat was followed by the fall of Fort Lee four days later, forcing Washington to flee with his army across the Jerseys in search of a new headquarters.

And that was just 1776. In 1777 Washington performed very poorly at the Battles of Brandywine and Germantown and failed to keep the British from occupying Philadelphia, the seat of the Continental Congress. Brandywine was particularly galling in that it came on the heels of the American victory at Saratoga and brought into stark contrast Washington's performance with that of the generals in the northern department. The loss resulted from Washington's inability to gather adequate intelligence—a dilemma not faced by his opponent. Fortunately for Washington, he was able to maneuver a respectful retreat and avoid a total drubbing. Germantown was a daring might-have-been that was spoiled from its complexity and poor execution. All told, Washington's weaknesses as a military commander were clearly exhibited in the first two years of the war.

100 But did Washington win some battles?

Yes. Harlem Heights was a good success because it showed for the first time that Washington's troops could stand close fire from the experienced regular British army. It was more a skirmish than a battle, but throughout the day the American troops put the "Enemy to flight in open Ground" and kept fighting "with great spirit and intrepidity" even after their commanding officers were killed. Resolute in the face of sizzling enemy fire and heavy casualties, "this little advantage has inspired our troops prodigiously," declared Washington. "They find it only requires resolution and good officers to make an enemy give way."

More dramatic were the Battles of Trenton and Princeton, Washington's daring raids on enemy encampments in New Jersey. They came on the heels of Washington's appalling showing on the battlefields in New York and subsequent retreat into Pennsylvania. Both he and his army were completely demoralized, and the relative safety of geography scarcely ensured the survival of his army since most of the troops' terms of enlistment were set to expire on the last day of 1776. Washington was on the verge of despair when he hit upon an audacious plan to attack the British army garrison at Trenton on Christmas Day. Crossing the ice-laden Delaware River took several hours longer than expected, and only one of the three planned crossings succeeded, but one was enough—the Americans completely surprised and surrounded the enemy, who failed to notice their approach until it was too late. Washington's troops suffered six casualties, only two of whom died, while the Hessians lost twenty-two killed, eighty-four wounded, and more than nine hundred captured.

The assault on Trenton was a brilliant success, and probably saved the American cause. Almost as impressive was the follow-up a week later, when Lord Cornwallis concentrated his troops at Trenton with the aims of engaging the Americans. Washington astutely guessed that the British stores had been left inadequately guarded at Princeton and decided to go after them. He slipped his army away in the dead of night, fooling the British by keeping alive his campfires and the sounds of entrenchments. Washington was able to enter Princeton after running over British resistance, and leave the area before Cornwallis was able to get his troops up.

101 Did Washington have other successes?

Yes, Yorktown, of course—the most important American victory. But before Yorktown there was Monmouth Courthouse, in June 1778, a battle claimed to have been won by both the British and the Americans. If it was a draw, it was one Washington would have settled for any time, for at the end of the day, when both armies withdrew from the field, American casualties amounted to about three hundred and sixty-five, whereas the British casualties were more than twelve hundred, half of whom were deserters. After Monmouth the British were less anxious to enter into combat with the Americans, and in fact it was the last major battle of the war to take place in the northern theater. Just as noteworthy, Washington's deportment at Monmouth solidified his reputation as a great military commander.

> *General Washington commanded in person on this memorable day. He was exposed to every danger while encouraging and animating his troops, and his presence and example were of the utmost importance during the day. After the action, at night, he laid down in his cloak under a tree, with the expectation of recommencing the battle in the morning, but the royal army silently retreated during the night without being pursued.*
> —James Thatcher, Journal entry, 1778

> *General Washington was never greater in battle than in this action. His presence stopped the retreat; his arrangements secured the victory. His graceful bearing on horseback, his calm and dignified deportment, which still retained some traces of the displeasure he had experienced in the morning, were all calculated to excite the highest degree of enthusiasm.*
> —Lafayette, *Memoirs, Correspondence and Manuscripts,* 1837

102 Did Washington curse at Monmouth?

We want to believe so, because the day demanded it. The object of his ire was Major General Charles Lee, who had been ordered to lead the assault against the rear guard of the British baggage train, stretched five miles through Monmouth County in its retreat to New York from Philadelphia. Lee did not prepare for the battle, however, and when the fighting started he issued a series of irrational orders and counter orders that resulted in a frenzied retreat of his troops. Washington rode onto the scene as Lee was retreating, and it was at that moment that he supposedly cursed Lee with stinging rebukes. Washington then single handedly rallied the men and turned the tide of the battle. It was not until many years later, however, that the report of Washington's cursing came to light, and it was in the context of the observer justifying his own habitual use of profanity.

> *Yes, sir, he did once. It was at Monmouth and on a day that would have made any man swear. Yes, sir, he swore that day till the leaves shook on the trees. Charming! Delightful! Never have I enjoyed such swearing before or since. Sir, on that memorable day he swore like an angel from heaven!*
> —Charles Scott, quoted in George Washington Parke Custis, *Recollections of Washington*, 1859

103 Was Yorktown a great victory?

If anything demonstrates the military prowess of George Washington, it was the siege and Battle of Yorktown, in 1781. Although he was headquartered in Newburgh, New York, Washington recognized the opportunity afforded to him by Cornwallis's abandonment of North Carolina and move into Virginia. Washington began making preparations to take advantage of what he considered a serious British blunder. He adroitly negotiated to bring in the French as allies, devising a joint land and sea operation of nearly twenty thousand troops—a force capable of overwhelming Cornwallis's command of ten thousand, four hundred. Then, before secretly marching his army down to the Chesapeake, Washington cleverly created diversionary forces in New York, where he had contemplated an attack on New York City. Finally, once the troops were in place, Washington arranged and directed the bombardment and final attack of the British redoubts. The outcome was a spectacular conquest that in effect brought to an end the hostilities between America and Britain.

104 Was there a Battle of Valley Forge?

No. Valley Forge, Pennsylvania, served as Washington's Continental army headquarters from December 1777 to June 1778.

105 Was Valley Forge as bad as it has been portrayed?

Yes, although the winter was actually milder than some of the other winters of the Revolutionary War. The reason that there was so much suffering at the Valley Forge encampment was because of the poor organization of the commissary department and a resulting lack of supplies. One officer noted that rations were so puny that "the Beef has no Fat and the Proportion of Bone so great that it does not suffice" and predicted that stealing and robbing would increase among the men, "if no other bad Consequences follow." Washington stayed with his men through the entire winter even as many other officers went home on furlough, earning him the respect and admiration of the common soldier. Despite the severe hardships associated with he encampment at Valley Forge, the Continental army stayed there because it was a natural defensive position not far from the British, then headquartered at Philadelphia.

> *It is with infinite pain & concern that I transmit Congress the inclosed Copies of Sundry Letters respecting the state of the Commissary's Department. In these matters are not exaggerated. I do not know from what cause this alarming deficiency, or rather total failure of Supplies arises: But unless more vigorous exertions and better regulations take place in that line and immediately, This Army must dissolve.*
> —George Washington to Henry Laurens, 1777

106 Did Washington have a vision at Valley Forge?

Not likely—but why let that get in the way of an good story?

Washington's Vision was a Northern American Civil War propaganda tract written by Charles Wesley Alexander under the pseudonym Wesley Bradshaw. Originally published as a one-page broadside in April 1861, the author purported to have met an elderly Revolutionary War soldier named Anthony Sherman who related a remarkable story given to him by George Washington. Sherman claimed that General Washington, while praying in his tent at Valley Forge, had been visited by mysterious shadowy angels who foretold of frightening events that would befall America. The angels revealed three great perils that the republic would have to face, three wars that would envelope America.

The first war, with Europe, symbolized the Revolutionary War. A beautiful female angel appeared before the astonished Washington, and after some time greeted him with the words, "Son of the Republic, look and learn." She then extended her arm to the east, revealing another angel, a dark, shadowy being floating in mid-air over Europe and America. The second angel sprinkled water from the ocean on America and Europe, and a cloud arose, covering America in its "murky folds. Sharp flashes of lightning gleamed through it at intervals, and I heard the smothered groans and cries of the American people." The angel then dipped and sprinkled more water from the ocean, the "heaving billows sank from view," and the American landscape was dotted from the Atlantic to the Pacific with towns and villages and cites.

The second war was the American Civil War. The mysterious voice resounded again, "Son of the Republic, the end of the century cometh, look and learn." Washington was then made aware of the second peril. "At this the dark shadowy angel turned his face southward, and from Africa I saw an ill-omened spectre approach our land. It flitted slowly over every town and city of the latter. The inhabitants presently set themselves in battle array against each other." After much bloodletting a bright angel with the word "Union" on its brow and bearing an American flag appeared and reminded the divided nation to "Remember ye are brethren." Suddenly the fighting stopped and the warring peoples rallied around the national standard.

The third war foretold was to occur in the unknown distant future. The same words demanded Washington's attention, "Son of the Republic, look and learn." From Europe, Asia, and Africa arose "thick, black clouds that were soon joined into one. And throughout this mass there gleamed a dark red light by which I saw hordes of armed men, who, moving with the cloud, marched by land and sailed by sea to America, which country was enveloped in the volume of cloud." Millions were engaged in mortal combat, and the land was devastated. Of the last war, the angel declared: "The most fearful is the third passing which the whole world united shall not prevail against her." The conflagration was halted only by the reappearance from heaven of the angel with the national flag, this time with sword in hand, "attended by legions of white spirits." The Americans, "well nigh overcome," took courage, renewed the battle, and became victorious.

The vision ended, but not before the angel declared to Washington one piece of good news. "While the stars remain, and the heavens send down dew upon the earth, so long shall the Union last." Alexander finishes the tract with Anthony Sherman declaring "Such, my friends, were the words I heard from Washington's own lips, and America will do well to profit by them."

Original broadsides of Alexander's *Washington's Vision* are extremely rare; only one or two copies are known to have survived. Alexander reprinted the story in 1864, however, and it has been reprinted several times since. It was popularized by printings in the newspapers of the Grand Army of the Republic, the *National Tribune* (1880), and the *Stars and Stripes* (1950). It was reprinted as an anti-communist tract by a Christian organization in Fairhope, Alabama, in the 1950s, and most widely circulated as a free gospel tract in the 1960s through the 1980s by the Pilgrim Tract Society of Randleman, North Carolina. (It is ironic that Christians have latched onto the story, when they typically believe Jesus' declaration that angels are neither male nor female, for both male and female angels appear to Washington.) It is the third peril that continued to give life to the tract in the twentieth century, with the threat of worldwide communism and the description of Washington seeing hordes of armed men through a gleaming "dark red light."

Charles Wesley Alexander (1837–1927) lived in Philadelphia and during the Civil War listed his occupations in city directories as clerk (1861), advertising agent (1862), reporter (1863), author (1864), and publisher (1865). When Alexander's *Washington's Vision* appeared in 1861 its readers readily understood its author's obvious allegiance to the North and the political implications of the use of the terms Republic and Union. Alexander's intention was to warn Americans that it was normal for republics to face perils, and that only the supremacy of the Union could ensure the permanent survival of the United States, which was then only seventy-five years old.

Alexander's subsequent wartime publication of two other single-page broadsides reinforced his reputation as a partisan Unionist. *Jeff Davis' Confession! A Singular Document Found on the Dead Body of a Rebel!* (1861), purports to be letter from Davis to the American People, in which the president of the Confederacy rationalizes the "injuries I have inflicted upon the American nation," and admits that he is "outlawed and forever ruined." *General McClellan's Dream* (1862) has Union army General George B. McClellan falling asleep at his desk only to be awakened by a vision of George Washington, who asked, "General McClellan, do you sleep at your post?" The agitated hero of the Revolution then warned the lethargic McClellan to act quickly, in order to prevent the Confederate army from capturing Washington, D.C.

Alexander also has been credited with creating a genre of stories about fictional Civil War heroines who—as women—joined the armed conflict as soldiers. Such included *Pauline of the Potomac* (1862), *Maud of the Mississippi* (1863), and *General Sherman's Indian Spy* (1865). At least one title, *The Picket Slayer* (1863), depicted a devilish young girl fighting for the Confederacy.

The bottom line? Angels might have visited George Washington at Valley Forge, but he never told anyone about it!

107 What was the Conway Cabal?

An attempt beginning in 1777 among some high-ranking Continental army officers and members of the Continental Congress to have Washington replaced as commander in chief. The cabal, which was not so much a conspiracy as an unorganized faction, takes its name from Major General Thomas Conway of the Continental army, a native of Ireland who was educated and reared in France. Conniving with Conway were Major General Horatio Gates, commander of the Continental army in the northern department, and two Signers of the Declaration of Independence, Thomas Mifflin, the former Continental quartermaster general and a member of Congress's Board of War, and Dr. Benjamin Rush, sometimes called the father of American medicine.

Indiscreet correspondence between the schemers led to their plot being made public, and Washington's supporters rallied to his side. Eventually both Conway and Gates were disgraced, Conway for his condescending tone to members of Congress, Gates because of the disastrous defeat of his army in Camden, South Carolina.

This was the unhappy condition of that army, on whom General Washington had to rely for the defence of every thing held most dear by Americans, and this, too, while situated within sixteen miles of a powerful adversary, with a greatly superior army of veterans, watching with a vigilant eye for an opportunity to effect its destruction. But a fact which excites the greatest indignation and astonishment is, that, at the critical period above mentioned, a party in Congress, in concert with General Conway, was endeavoring to remove General Washington from the supreme command. If the American army is to be annihilated, and the cause of our country sacrificed to gratify individual ambition, then is there a faction ripe for the execution of the object. No man, perhaps, ever had a greater combination of vexatious evils and uncontrollable obstacles to encounter, than this incomparable patriot

*and warrior; and no one surely ever possessed in a more
eminent degree the peculiar talents and qualities requisite
for the discharge of the important duties assigned him in
his elevated station. He has acquired the full confidence of
every faithful officer and soldier under his command, and
his wisdom and judgment are considered adequate to the
most trying exigencies. He rises in the midst of distress,
and gains strength by misfortunes.*
— James Thatcher, Journal entry, 1778

108 Why is Washington called America's first spymaster?

Washington learned the value of good intelligence during the French and Indian War when hundreds of miles of wilderness separated him and his troops from their military staging areas. When he took command of the Continental army in 1775 Washington was well aware that the British still entertained strong support across the colonies, and that many Loyalists were eager to feed information to the British. At first Washington tended to have his spies report directly to himself, but soon he saw the necessity of setting in place a real espionage network.

*We have the greatest Occasion at present for hard
Money, to pay a certain set of People who are of particular
use to us. If you could possibly collect a Sum, if it were but
One hundred or one hundred and fifty Pounds it would be
of great Service. Silver would be most convenient.*
— George Washington to Robert Morris, 1776

Even so, Washington kept the members of his spy rings very close to his own chest. He assigned code numbers to each, keeping their identities hidden from one another; his own number was 711. He only used men that he thought could be trusted, paying them in hard currency. His espionage methods included the use of surveillance, disinformation, pseudonyms, dead drops, codes, and invisible ink (developed by a brother of John Jay, later chief justice). Despite the best efforts of Washington and his network of spies, the intelligence was sometimes faulty.

Some of Washington's more famous spies included: Thomas Knowlton, a Massachusetts patriot placed in charge of the first American special forces, Knowlton's Rangers; Nathan Hale, the Connecticut school teacher hanged by the British in New York and legendary for his last words, "I only regret that I have but one life to lose for my country"; Haym Salomon, a Jewish merchant who had fled persecution from his native Poland and who twice barely escaped execution by the British for spying; Hercules Mulligan, a New York haberdasher and close friend of Alexander Hamilton; Staten Islanders Joshua Mersereau and his sons Joshua, Jr., and John; merchant Robert Townsend; John Honeyman, a Scots-Irish weaver from New Jersey who posed as a Tory; Daniel Bissell, a fake deserter later awarded the Purple Heart for his efforts; Abraham Patten, executed after the burning of New York City; paroled New Jersey prisoner Lewis Costigin, known as "Z" (whose identity was not even revealed to Washington); and Benjamin Tallmadge, Washington's chief spy organizer.

> *There can be scarce any need of recommending the greatest caution and secrecy in a business so critical and dangerous; the following seem to be best general Rules: To entrust none but the persons fixed upon to transact the Business; to deliver the dispatches to none upon our side but to those who shall be pitched upon for the purpose of receiving them and to transmit them and any verbal intelligence that may be obtained to no one but the Commander in Chief.*
> —George Washington, Instructions
> for C– Senior and C– Junior, 1779

109 Did Washington order his spies to burn New York City in 1776?

Washington denied doing so, although he had advocated destroying the city rather than giving it over to enemy occupiers. The fire could have been an accident, but British and Loyalist observers laid the conflagration at the feet of rebel arsonists, claiming that fires broke in several places at once. They also claimed to have apprehended a number of miscreants in the act of starting fires and obstructing firefighting efforts, and to have discovered accelerants concealed for further acts of mischief. Local firefighters tended to confirm such suspicions.

The British did not immediately conduct an investigation into the burning of New York City, and those accused of setting fires either went free or were punished without due process. Eventually, blame for the fire was cast not only on American Patriots but on British and Hessian troops as well. For his part, Washington insisted the fire was an accident, and that once started the British failed to do all they could to extinguish it.

> *Had I been left to the dictates of my own judgment, New York should have been laid in Ashes before I quitted it; to this end I applied to Congress, but was absolutely forbid; that they will have cause to repent the Order, I have not a moments doubt of, nor never had, as it was obvious to me (covered as it may be by their ships) that it will be next to impossible for us to dispossess them of it again as all their Supplies come by Water, whilst ours were derived by Land; besides this, by leaving it standing, the Enemy are furnished with warm and comfortable Barracks, in which their whole Force may be concentred, the place secured by a small garrison (if they chuse it) having their ships round it, and only a narrow Neck of Land to defend, and their principal force left at large to act against us, or to remove to any other place for the purpose of harrassing us. this in my judgment may be set down amg. one of the capitol errors of Congress. . . . In speaking of New York, I had*

forgot to mention that Providence, or some good honest Fellow, has done more for us than we were disposed to do for ourselves, as near One fourth of the City is supposed to be consumed. however enough of it remains to answer their purposes.

—George Washington to
Lund Washington, 1776

110 Who was Washington's best general?

Without doubt, Nathanael Greene, of Rhode Island. Henry Knox, Washington's artillery commander and an outstanding general himself, said that within the first year of the Revolutionary War, Greene transformed himself from "the rawest, the most untutored being," into the finest general officer in the Continental army. By that time, Washington believed that if he were captured or killed that Greene should succeed him as commander in chief of the American forces. Washington demonstrated his confidence in Greene by placing him in charge of the entire army for a few days in August 1777 while Washington reconnoitered the American fortifications along the Delaware River.

General Greene has conducted in a manner to meet the expectations and full approbation of the public, and has been promoted to the rank of major-general. By his military talents, skill and judgment, he has acquired a character of the highest order, and is held in respect and estimation throughout the army, as second only to the commander-in-chief. It is the prevailing sentiment, that if in any event of Providence we should be deprived of our chief commander, General Greene is of all others the most suitable character to be his successor and in this sentiment there is the greatest reason to believe that the illustrious Washington himself would readily coincide.

—James Thatcher, Journal entry, 1780

Washington and Greene were much alike. Neither had much of a formal education, and both excelled in mathematics. Both were athletic and enjoyed social events, especially balls and dancing. Each used their talents, wit, and determination to climb the social and economic ladders of their day. Both were elected to provincial legislatures at a young age, and both became political radicals who early on expected the colonies to separate from Great Britain. Each felt a strong sense of duty and each was convinced that their pursuits were aligned with what was right. A perceptive nineteenth-century historian noted that Greene's "almost intuitive perception of character" resembled Washington's. Greene, like Washington, "seemed to take the exact measure of every man who approached him."

Greene made valuable contributions to the American war effort. Early on he assisted Washington in planning military campaigns, and he took lead roles in directing the operations. He rearranged the quartermaster department beginning in 1778, and in 1780 he was appointed commander of the southern department. Greene's famous retreat across the Carolinas into Virginia in 1781 set the stage for Washington's trapping Cornwallis at Yorktown, and after Cornwallis left off the chase, Greene began a "war of posts" aimed at clearing the British out of the Carolinas and Georgia.

111 What about Benedict Arnold?

The most notorious traitor in American history was once a favorite of George Washington. Arnold played an instrumental role in capturing the arms-rich garrison at Ticonderoga, New York, and Washington supported his bid to lead an expedition against Quebec. When Arnold succeeded in making the march through the northern wilderness, Washington praised his efforts. The capture of Quebec proved elusive, but Arnold still provided a valuable service in the north by constructing a fleet to fight the British on Lake Champlain. Washington asked the Continental Congress to promote Arnold for the feat, but Congress failed to act until Arnold again showed his worth by defending the military stores at Danbury, Connecticut, in April 1777.

It is not in the power of any man to command success, but you have done more—you have deserved it, & before this I hope, have met with the Laurels which are due to your Toils, in the possession of Quebec—My thanks are due, & sincerely offered to you, for your Enterprizing & perservering spirit.
　　—George Washington to Benedict Arnold, 1775

Arnold showed his merit yet again in September 1777 when British General John Burgoyne's forces were captured. He was badly wounded in the leg and forced to convalesce in a hospital for five months, yet his sacrifice was hardly noticed—except by Washington who commended his courage and conduct with a set of epaulettes and sword-knots recently sent from France. When the British evacuated Philadelphia a few months later, Washington placed the city under Arnold's command. That move proved disastrous, however, for once he was in Philadelphia Arnold quarreled endlessly with members of Congress.

Washington knew that Arnold was unhappy and offered him a wing command in the campaign of 1780, but Arnold declined, saying his leg prevented it. Washington then appointed him commander of West Point. What Washington did not know was that Arnold already had entered into a treasonous correspondence with Major John André of the British army. The unexpected capture of André revealed that Arnold was about to give the West Point garrison to the British. The unsuspecting Washington was livid, of course, and supported attempts to capture Arnold alive—but he was never apprehended. To Americans the former friends came to represent the best and the worst of men, the embodiment of perfidy and virtue.

112 Did Washington stop an officers' mutiny during the war?

Yes. In the final years of the war, after Yorktown, the army was still in the field but it was not being paid, owing to the dismal state of the Continental treasury. Officers and soldiers alike complained, but to no avail. Finally, in March 1783, at Newburgh, New York, where Washington was headquartered, an anonymous address called on the officers to meet to "redress their own grievances." The writer of the address proposed that Congress be given an ultimatum: meet our demands or the officers will instead of disbanding the army at the end of the war take the army to some unsettled country. This was cause for concern, especially given eighteenth-century fears of a standing army.

When Washington learned of the address he forbade the officers to assemble. Nevertheless, he was sympathetic to their plight and wisely turned around and convened a meeting at which they could express their discontent. At first, Washington did not plan to attend, but then he changed his mind; so his appearance at the meeting was unexpected. Once in the room with the officers he began making remarks, and then pulled out of his pocket a letter from a delegate to Congress. He began to read the letter, so haltingly that he reached into his pocket for his spectacles, commenting while doing so, "Gentlemen, you must pardon me. I have grown gray in your service and now find myself growing blind." It was a simple remark and before the assembled officers could hardly take it in Washington departed the scene. The effect was momentous, however, and the officers then passed resolutions expressing confidence in Congress and rejecting "with disdain" the Newburgh Addresses. The mutiny was over, but the Newburgh Conspiracy, so-called, did wake up Congress—a few days afterward it promised the officers five years pay in lieu of the half-pay pensions already approved but not appropriated.

113 Did Washington design the Purple Heart at Newburgh?

Yes. In fact, Washington devised two honorary badges of distinction while at Newburgh, which he announced in General Orders in August 1782. The first was a chevron for enlisted men and noncommissioned officers of the Continental army who had served more than three years with "bravery, fidelity and good conduct." The design was a narrow white stripe to be worn on the left coat sleeve, or two stripes for those who had completed more than six years. The second badge, the Purple Heart, was to be awarded for the performance of "any singularly meritorious action." The figure of a heart cut from purple cloth and edged with narrow silver lace was to be worn on the facing of the uniform, over the left breast. Names of the awardees would be enrolled in a Book of Merit.

Washington awarded the Purple Heart only three times, and all three recipients were Connecticut sergeants: Elijah Churchill, William Brown, and Daniel Bissell, Jr. No other American soldiers were so honored until 1932, when in honor of the bicentennial of Washington's birth, President Herbert Hoover asked General Douglas MacArthur to reintroduce the Badge of Military Merit to honor those wounded or killed in the line of duty in World War I. MacArthur kept the motif of a purple heart, turning it into a medal with Washington's portrait in the center. MacArthur, who had been wounded in battle, was granted the first Purple Heart medal.

> *Honorary Badges of distinction are to be conferred on the veteran Non commissioned officers and soldiers of the army who have served more than three years with bravery, fidelity and good conduct; for this purpose a narrow piece of white cloath of an angular form is to be fixed to the left arm on the uniform Coat. Non commissioned officers and soldiers who have served with equal reputation more than six years are to be distinguished by two pieces of cloth set in parellel to each other in a simular form; should any*

who are not entitled to these honors have the insolence to assume the badges of them they shall be severely punished. On the other hand it is expected those gallant men who are thus designated will on all occasions be treated with particular confidence and consideration.

The General ever desirous to cherish virtuous ambition in his soldiers, as well as to foster and encourage every species of Military merit, directs that whenever any singularly meritorious action is performed, the author of it shall be permitted to wear on his facings over the left breast, the figure of a heart in purple cloth, or silk, edged with narrow lace or binding. Not only instances of unusual gallantry, but also of extraordinary fidelity and essential service in any way shall meet with a due reward. Before this favour can be conferred on any man, the particular fact, or facts, on which it is to be grounded must be set forth to the Commander in chief accompanied with certificates from the Commanding officers of the regiment and brigade to which the Candadate for reward belonged, or other incontestable proofs, and upon granting it, the name and regiment of the person with the action so certified are to be enrolled in the book of merit which will be kept at the orderly office. Men who have merited this last distinction to be suffered to pass all guards and sentinals which officers are permitted to do.

The road to glory in a patriot army and a free country is thus open to all. This order is also to have retrospect to the earliest stages of the war, and to be considered as a permanent one.

—George Washington, General Orders, 1782

114 Did Washington turn down a chance to become King of the United States?

It is a commonly held belief that George Washington could have been king of the United States, rather than its first president. Nothing could have been further from Washington's own mind, however.

Washington firmly believed in civilian rule, not military or monarchial, and always submitted both himself and the Continental army to the civilian authority of the Continental Congress, even after Congress granted him dictatorial powers in 1777. Washington fully supported the Declaration of Independence, which faulted King George III for the American grievances with Great Britain. While it is true that Loyalists abounded in America during the Revolution and that pro-monarchical sentiments were common even among a segment of the Continental army, both Washington and the Continental Congress waged war based on republican principles. During the war, especially after it became clear that the Americans had beaten the British militarily, few, if any, of the political leaders of the various states were willing to betray those ideals—especially George Washington.

Washington was aware of his own role in history. He consciously modeled himself after two great republican leaders of ancient Rome— Cincinnatus, the farmer who left his plow in the field to become a soldier when Rome was threatened, only to lay down his sword and return to his plow when his country no longer needed him; and Cato the Younger—like Washington renowned for his honesty—who thought suicide more honorable than submission to the tyranny of Julius Caesar. One further reason that Washington did not favor a hereditary monarchy was personal: He had no natural-born children.

The basis of the story that Washington was offered the chance to become king is a letter that Lewis Nicola, a former British army officer and colonel of the Continental army Invalid Regiment, wrote to Washington in May 1782. In the letter, Nicola advocated the creation of a new state with a limited constitutional monarchy on the "best of those fruitful & extensive countries to the west of our frontiers"—with Washington at its helm. Nicola justified his proposal by calling attention to the inefficiency of the Continental Congress in prosecuting the war effort and Congress's inability to pay its soldiers and other debts. Nicola said that he was not a "violent admirer of a republican form of government"—a statement that surely caused ire in Washington, an early radical proponent of the Revolution. Tempering his language somewhat, Nicola asserted that it "must not be concluded from this that I am a partisan for absolute monarchy." Rather, Nicola declared himself a proponent of "limited, suppose not hereditary" monarchy, in which the king would not control the nation's purse strings. Nicola suggested that the new state might give the head of the government some title "more moderate" than king, although he hoped not.

Washington was greatly offended by Nicola's proposal, and told him so in an immediate reply, written on 22 May 1782. Nicola responded to Washington's reaction with three separate letters of apology for his "erroneous" "opinion on different forms of government." "However wrong the sentiments I have disclosed to your Excellency may be," Nicola wrote in one of his apologies, "they cannot have done any mischief, as they have always remained locked up in my breast."

Nineteenth-century historians believed that Nicola spoke for a faction of the army, in Jared Sparks's words, that was "neither small in number, nor insignificant in character." They also tended to conflate the Nicola affair with the ensuing Newburgh Conspiracy, which Washington personally squelched upon learning of the intrigues of some high-ranking army officers to set up military rule—with him at their head. The fact is, however, that Nicola represented no such faction and spoke only for himself, even if others in the army did harbor similar sentiments—Washington in 1788 when asked about the Nicola letter did intimate that "there were several applications made to me" of a similar nature. No one knew better than Washington himself, however, that the republican experiment demanded republican leaders.

> Sir: With a mixture of great surprise and astonishment
> I have read with attention the Sentiments you have
> submitted to my perusal. Be assured Sir, no occurrence in
> the course of the War, has given me more painful sensations
> than your information of there being such ideas existing

*in the Army as you have expressed, and I must view with
abhorrence, and reprehend with severity. For the present,
the communication of them will rest in my own bosom,
unless some further agitation of the matter, shall make a
disclosure necessary.*

*I am much at a loss to conceive what part of my conduct
could have given encouragement to an address which to
me seems big with the greatest mischiefs that can befall my
Country. If I am not deceived in the knowledge of myself,
you could not have found a person to whom your schemes
are more disagreeable; at the same time in justice to my
own feelings I must add, that no Man possesses a more
sincere wish to see ample justice done to the Army than I do,
and as far as my powers and influence, in a constitutional
way extend, they shall be employed to the utmost of my
abilities to effect it, should there be any occasion. Let me
conjure you then, if you have any regard for your Country,
concern for yourself or posterity, or respect for me, to banish
these thoughts from your Mind, and never communicate,
as from yourself, or any one else, a sentiment of the like
Nature.*

—George Washington to Lewis Nicola, 1782

115 Did Washington support the United States Constitution?

Yes. Washington thought long and hard before lending his name
to the Constitutional Convention with his attendance. Although
he believed the union of states needed a strong central government,
he was skeptical that a "general Convention" could make up the
deficiencies of the national government that existed under the Articles
of Confederation. Yet he believed something had to be done or the
fabric of government would begin to unravel. He spent months
deliberating the matter of the upcoming Constitutional Convention
in Philadelphia before finally deciding to attend as a member of the
Virginia delegation.

> *It is too probable that no plan we propose will be adopted. Perhaps another dreadful conflict is to be sustained. If, to please the people, we offer what we ourselves disprove, how can we afterwards defend our work? Let us raise a standard to which the wise and the honest can repair. The event is in the hand of God.*
>
> —George Washington, Opening Remarks to the United States Constitutional Convention, 1787

Washington's presence in Philadelphia legitimized the Convention's proceedings, and the proposed Constitution. He was unanimously elected president of the Convention but took almost no part in the ensuing debates. His voting record with the Virginia delegation, however, reveals that he was an advocate of a strong national government and a strong executive office. The high esteem that he was held in by his fellow delegates is revealed by the fact that they entrusted the Convention's papers to his care.

> *I think that, were it not for one great character in America, so many men would not be for this government. We have one ray of hope. We do not fear while he lives; but we can only expect his* fame *to be immortal. We wish to know who, besides him, can concentrate the confidence and affections of all America.*
>
> —William Grayson, Virginia Ratification Convention, 1788

At the conclusion of the Convention, Washington said that the Constitution was the best that could have emerged under the circumstances. He was satisfied that the general government was given power sufficient to perform the necessary functions of government but that those powers were under enough checks and balances to keep the system from "degenerating into a monarchy, an Oligarchy, an Aristocracy, or any other despotic or oppressive form." "Nor am I yet such an enthusiastic, partial or undiscriminating admirer of it," he wrote Lafayette, "as not to perceive it is tinctured with some real (though not radical) defects." But, in his words, "we are not to expect perfection in this world," and he thus was pleased when the Constitution was ratified by the states.

> *Be assured, his influence carried this government.*
> —James Monroe to Thomas Jefferson, 1787

116 Is it true that Washington was not the first president?

No. While many adamantly believe this to be true, it is based on a misunderstanding of the history of how the United States government came into being. The Declaration of Independence dissolved the political connection between the thirteen American colonies and Great Britain, declaring that those colonies were "Free and Independent States, they have full Power to levy War, conclude Peace, contract Alliances, establish Commerce, and to do all other Acts and Things which Independent States may of right do." Throughout the Revolutionary War these states each governed independently under their own system, although they chose to work together in the Continental Congresses. The ratification of the Articles of Confederation in 1781 created not the government of the United States but a *new alliance* of the thirteen independent and sovereign states that would send representatives to a new national Congress. These states did not give up their independence or autonomy and the central government was subordinated to them. Under the Articles of Confederation the central government had no executive or judicial branches, or powers to tax or raise an army. Washington described the Confederation government as "little more than the shadow without substance."

According to this erroneous line of reasoning, Washington was not the first but the eleventh president, preceded by Samuel Huntington, Thomas McKean, John Hanson, Elias Boudinot, Thomas Mifflin, Richard Henry Lee, John Hancock, Nathan Gorman, Arthur St. Clair, and Cyrus Griffin—all presidents under the Articles of Confederation, between 1781 and the inauguration of Washington. (Some argue that John Hanson, the third president under the Articles, should be considered the first Confederation president as neither Huntington nor McKean completed a full one-year term). If this reasoning is stretched to its logical conclusion, the first president was actually Peyton Randolph, elected president of the First Continental Congress in 1774, and Washington the fifteenth person to hold the office. (Randolph's successors in the Continental Congress included Henry Middleton, John Hancock, Henry Laurens, John Jay, and Samuel Huntington). In fact, all these men except Washington were presiding officers of the various Congresses, Continental and Confederation, and no one at the time considered any of these men excepting Washington as anything but president of Congress. Washington, as chief of the executive branch under the Constitution, in fact presided over nothing.

Along the same lines is another misunderstanding, that Washington was not born in America. According to this line of reasoning not only Washington but United States Presidents John Adams, Thomas Jefferson, James Madison, James Monroe, John Quincy Adams, and Andrew Jackson also were not born in America, and Martin Van Buren, born 1782, was the first president born in the United States. While it may be accurate to say that Washington and the next six presidents were not born in the United States but in one of the British-American colonies, it is not true that these colonies were not considered to be America by the people of Great Britain. America is a continent and was so named and known by Europeans more than two hundred and fifty years before the establishment of the United States government.

The United States Constitution, adopted at the Convention over which Washington presided, explicitly states that "No person except a natural born citizen, or a citizen of the United States, at the time of the adoption of this Constitution, shall be eligible to the office of President" (Article II, Section 1).

117 Did Washington campaign for president?

No. During the Constitutional Convention the office of the presidency was designed with Washington's example in mind, and he considered it more a burden than an honor to serve as president. Washington abhorred political factions, about which he warned the country in his Farewell Address, and although he did allow his name to be put forward by his friends, Washington, like other gentlemen in the eighteenth century, did not actively campaign for political office. Imagine Washington running a non-campaign for president today!

118 Why did Washington accept the presidency if he considered it a burden?

Although the Americans had prevailed over the British in a protracted war, Washington knew the union of states was precariously weak and that to survive it needed a strong central government with a strong chief executive at its helm. He also knew that Americans fundamentally distrusted government and strong executives, and that the representatives in the Constitutional Convention had designed the executive department with his example in mind. Hence, Washington was willing to let the country rally around him much as he done during the Revolutionary War.

119 What were Washington's goals as president?

They were threefold: First, he wanted to establish a federal government powerful enough to administer domestic affairs to the satisfaction of the people in all thirteen states and to command the respect of foreign nations. Second, he wanted to put the country's finances on a solid footing by protecting the government's credit and paying off the Revolutionary War debts. Third, he wanted to manage foreign affairs in a manner consistent with the interests of the American people. Ancillary to these goals was the establishment and design of the Federal City on the banks of the Potomac River.

120 Did Washington create a strong executive branch?

Yes. Considering that eighteenth-century Americans were suspicious of executive authority, Washington's first goal may have been the most difficult to achieve, at least at the beginning. Washington's reputation for integrity and his unwavering resolve to keep his political conduct "exceedingly circumspect" won over the populace, however. He conducted himself and his household with the decorum fitting a republican head of state but shunned the ostentatious frills of monarchy. He conscientiously deferred to the prerogatives of Congress even as he molded the executive branch into a fundamentally powerful seat within the confines of the Constitution. And he avoided patronage by astutely balancing sectional and local interests when making some four hundred federal appointments during his presidency.

It is the nature of Republicans, who are nearly in a state of equality, to be extremely jealous as to the disposal of all honorary or lucrative appointments.
—George Washington to Samuel Vaughan, 1789

121 Did Washington have an economic plan?

No, but his concern for the country's finances was well placed. The war debts amounted to about seventy-five million dollars, two-thirds of which was owed by the federal government and the remainder by the states. (About eleven million was owed to Dutch financiers and the French government.) The annual interest on the total debt was far greater than the amount of revenue that would come into the federal treasury, and neither excessive taxation nor repudiation of the debts were considered as viable ways to retire the debt.

Washington did not attempt to develop an economic plan of his own but instead supported a brilliant but convoluted proposal devised by his secretary of the treasury, Alexander Hamilton. The plan's components included refinancing the debts at standard interest rates; assumption of all the debts by the federal government; placing custom duties on some imports and instituting an excise tax on domestically distilled spirits; and the creation of a national bank. Upon implementation Hamilton's complex plan proved an immediate success.

122 What was Washington's foreign policy?

United States foreign policy in Washington's day, like now, meant balancing the interests of the nation with the interests of other countries. Sometimes these interests converged but just as often they did not. Washington's view was that it was in the best interest of the United States to keep disentangled from the affairs of foreign nations, especially when those nations were in competition with one another.

After emerging victorious in the long struggle with Great Britain, maintaining the peace was of primary importance. The British were not anxious to live up to their promise to relinquish control of a line of military posts in the Northwest Territory, and Britain's continued occupation of those forts seriously curtailed American influence on the Indians along the western frontier. At the same time, Spain controlled the Mississippi River, New Orleans and the province of Louisiana, and East and West Florida. Allied with the Spanish was the Creek Nation, and to the Creeks Washington turned his attention, concluding a treaty in 1790. A second treaty followed in 1791, with the Cherokee Nation, proving that Washington was capable of negotiating treaties with foreign powers, but it was not until 1795—after the routing of Indian forces in the Ohio country—and proving that the United States had some military muscle—that Spain gave up its demands on the eastern side of the Mississippi and opened the great river to American commerce.

Washington's combined diplomatic and military triumphs were further buttressed by the ratification of the hotly contested Jay Treaty, the collapse of the Whiskey Rebellion, and his foresight regarding the French Revolution.

123 Why did Washington distrust the French Revolution?

Washington did support France's move toward republicanism but he feared that its efforts to reform government might go too far and slide into mayhem and cruelty—what proved to be an all-too-accurate assessment. At the same time, France's attempts to pull America into its war with Great Britain threatened United States neutrality at a time when Washington felt that his newborn government was too vulnerable to risk entering into another war, so soon after the conclusion of the Revolution.

124 What was Washington's Proclamation of Neutrality?

In April 1793 Washington formally issued a statement declaring the United States neutral in the war between France and Great Britain, and threatened to prosecute any American who engaged in the war on either side. Congress reinforced Washington's proclamation the following year with its Neutrality Act of 1794. Meanwhile, the new French envoy Edmund Genet had arrived in America and begun to actively interfere with American neutrality, confirming Washington's prognostications and alienating many Americans in the process.

125 What was the uproar over the Jay Treaty?

While the French were insisting that the United States become its ally in its war against Great Britain, the British were threatening to drag America into the war by interfering with American shipping on the high seas. Wishing to avoid war, Washington accordingly sent Chief Justice John Jay to London as special envoy to secretly negotiate with the British. While Jay failed to achieve all that Washington had hoped, the resulting Treaty of London of 1794 averted war with Great Britain and obtained the withdrawal of the British from the

Northwest Territory, as promised eleven years earlier. Concessions on both sides opened up trade and commerce between the former foes, and boundary disputes were sent into arbitration.

Nevertheless, many in America were unhappy that the negotiations had been conducted in secret, and those inclined toward France were particularly infuriated. The Jay Treaty crystallized the sharp contrasts of America's emerging political factions, personified in Thomas Jefferson and Alexander Hamilton. The Senate eventually ratified the Jay Treaty and Washington signed it, and by it the United States secured a badly needed decade of peace with Great Britain.

126   Was the Whiskey Rebellion about whiskey?

Not really. Simply put, it was a tax rebellion by backcountry settlers on the western frontiers of the middle and southern states. It began when Congress passed into law the fiscal plan drafted by Secretary of the Treasury Alexander Hamilton during Washington's first presidential administration, placing an excise tax on domestically distilled spirits. The settlers naturally opposed it because it interfered with the most efficient way of transporting grain to eastern markets. Opposition festered for two years before tensions came to a head in the summer of 1794, when tax officers were threatened with violence. The insurrection fizzled that fall, however, when a military force of nearly thirteen thousand men under the command of President Washington, Alexander Hamilton, and Light-Horse Harry Lee took to the field in Pennsylvania.

127   What was Washington's role in establishing the Federal City?

Washington was a great booster of the Federal City and kept abreast of its progress from the temporary seat of government in Philadelphia, visiting the site whenever he was able to travel to Mount Vernon. Washington promoted commercial development of the area, buying building lots both for investment purposes and to show his confidence in the city's future. He gave advice about the architectural style of the individual buildings, and assisted the commissioners in searching for skilled workers. Washington's greatest contribution to the Federal City, however, may have been his brokering of disagreements between the commissioners and L'Enfant and between the commissioners themselves.

Article 1, section 8, of the United States Constitution mandated the establishment of a permanent seat for the federal government, officially designated as the District of Columbia. The choice of the site on the Potomac River resulted from a political bargain between Washington's secretaries of state and treasury, Thomas Jefferson and Alexander Hamilton, in 1790. Although Washington preferred the Potomac—near his beloved Mount Vernon—he did not take part in the negotiations, which were handled by James Madison, at that time a member of the House of Representatives. After constituents from various sections of the country worked through their political, geographical, and economic concerns, Congress narrowly passed the Residence Act of 1790, locating the seat of government on a ten-mile-square area on the Potomac. Other locations considered included New York City, Philadelphia, and sites along the Susquehanna and Delaware Rivers. Provisions of the Residence Act included a ten-year development plan, and Washington died before the federal government relocated to the banks of the Potomac.

Washington's role in the establishment of the Federal City arose from provisions in the Resident Act that authorized the president to appoint commissioners to oversee the selection and acquisition of the specific site and the construction of public works. Washington worked closely with the commissioners, the United States surveyor general, and the chief architect and engineer, French-born Pierre-Charles L'Enfant.

The federal City in the year 1800 will become the seat of the general Government of the United States. It is encreasing fast in buildings, and rising into consequence; and will, I have no doubt, from the advantages given to it by nature, and its proximity to a rich interior country,

*and the western territory, become the emporium of the
United States.*
—George Washington to Arthur Young, 1793

128 Did Washington live in the White House?

No, the White House was incomplete during Washington's administration. In fact, during his two terms Washington did not even live in the Federal City—the temporary seats of the federal government were first New York City and then Philadelphia. John Adams was the first president to actually live in the White House, moving there in 1800.

A long-standing but unsubstantiated tradition is that the White House is named after the Custis plantation in New Kent County, where George and Martha were married.

129 Did Washington ever meet another head of state?

Actually, yes, although not the heads of European powers. In the French and Indian War, as early as 1753, Washington treated with two prominent chiefs of the Six Nations, the Half-King, an important Seneca chief allied with the British against the French in the Ohio Country, and his successor, Monacatoocha. (The Half-King christened Washington Conotocarious, meaning "town taker" or "devourer of villages," the same Indian name bestowed on Washington's great-grandfather John Washington.) During the Revolutionary War, Washington entertained a delegation of Delaware Indian chiefs at his Continental army headquarters in New Jersey. These meetings set the precedents for how Washington would negotiate with Indian sachems during his presidency.

*Our brigade was paraded for the purpose of being
reviewed by General Washington and a number of Indian
chiefs. His excellency, with his usual dignity, followed by*

his mulatto servant Bill, riding a beautiful gray steed, passed in front of the line, and received the salute. He was accompanied by a singular group of savages, whose appearance was beyond description ludicrous. Their horses were of the meanest kind, some of them destitute of saddles, and old lines were used for bridles. Their personal decorations were equally farcical, having their faces painted of various colors, jewels suspended from their ears and nose, their heads without covering, except tufts of hair on the crown, and some of them wore dirty blankets over their shoulders waving in the wind. In short, they exhibited a novel and truly disgusting spectacle. But his excellency deems it good policy to pay some attention to this tribe of the wilderness, and to convince them of the strength and discipline of our army, that they may be encouraged, if disposed to be friendly, or deterred from aggression, if they should become hostile to our country.

—James Thatcher, Journal entry, 1779

The most famous meetings between Washington and Indian heads of state took place in 1790, in New York and Philadelphia. In July and August, Washington and his cabinet lavishly received the principle chief of the Creek Indian nation, Alexander McGillivray, accompanied by twenty-three lesser chiefs who had traveled from Georgia to New York City. After direct negotiations a treaty ensued, as well as an appointment for McGillivray as United States agent to the Creeks with the rank of brigadier general, at an annual salary of fifteen hundred dollars. In December 1790 and January 1791, shortly after the seat of the federal government had moved to Philadelphia, Washington treated with three Seneca chiefs, Cornplanter, the principle chief, his brother Half-Town, and the Great-Tree. The negotiations resulted in Washington agreeing to offer protection to the Iroquois people from incursions by United States citizens.

130 Did Washington deliver his Farewell Address?

No, it was a written document circulated in primary newspapers throughout the country. The Farewell Address was Washington's public announcement to the people of the United States, that he would not seek a third term as president, and would retire altogether from public life. More importantly, the address served as a vehicle for Washington to relate his parting advice to his countrymen. It is an articulate statement of his political philosophy, developed over forty-five years of public service. Couched in language that warns and exhorts at the same time, Washington focused his attention on the principles of American government and the long-term future of the United States.

131 What are the themes of the Farewell Address?

Woven throughout the address is the central theme of perpetual union or the supremacy of national unity, based on the primacy of the Constitution. Warnings to steer clear of sectional and political divisions buttress his main theme. Further advice delineates how the United States should conduct foreign relations; the role of religion, morality, and education in public life; and the need to protect public credit and stabilize commercial and manufacturing interests.

132 Who wrote Washington's Farewell Address?

Washington drafted the Farewell Address with help from James Madison and Alexander Hamilton. Madison made the initial draft near the end of Washington's first presidential administration, when Washington seriously considered retiring from the presidency. After Washington decided to serve a second term he laid aside Madison's draft. In 1796 Washington sent Madison's draft to Hamilton, who incorporated only a part of it in a new draft. About one-third of the final address was based on Madison's original work.

Washington took an active part in drafting the Farewell Address. He provided its initial themes, took part in discussions with Madison and Hamilton about its ideas and how to express them, and refashioned its language to reflect his own writing style. In the end the final manuscript bears his unmistaken stamp. When the Farewell Address was printed in the Philadelphia *American Daily Advertiser* (it was not a spoken address) it was exactly as Washington had originally intended.

> *My wish is that the whole may appear in a plain style, and be handed to the public in an honest, unaffected, simple part.*

—George Washington to
Alexander Hamilton, 1796

133 Was Washington a great president?

Yes, in many ways the greatest, because, after all, he invented the office. The delegates to the Constitutional Convention had Washington in view when they created the office of chief executive, and upon his inauguration Washington immediately set about putting his stamp on the presidency. Washington wanted to make the presidency a strong, effective, and respected office, one deserving an international reputation, and in a few short years he managed to do so. But remember, he began his first term with only a handful of people in the executive branch and no examples to follow.

Washington appointed to his cabinet men of the highest caliber and made several hundred judicious federal appointments, carefully balancing political and sectional interests in the process. With the able assistance of those in his administration he solved the nation's debt crisis, secured the country's borders, either cajoled or forced neighboring Indian nations into peaceful compliance, and steered clear of the wars that raged in Europe—all in the context and confines of the Constitution, the law, and the prerogatives of Congress.

It was Washington's conviction that the public had invested its trust in him personally because of his reputation as an honest and disinterested public servant. He knew that the eyes of the nation were upon him, and he was careful of how his conduct might be interpreted by the public. Washington routinely sought counsel from his advisors, and he invariably made his decisions according to his best judgment and conscience. Well aware of the precedents that he was setting as a republican head of state, he was able to steer clear of the trappings of monarchy while molding the office into a fundamentally powerful one. Although over time political enemies emerged who opposed Washington's federalist leanings, the American populace never lost faith in his integrity or honesty or his commitment to the American experiment.

> *The powers of the Executive of the U. States are more definite, and better understood perhaps than those of almost any other Country; and my aim has been, and will continue to be, neither to stretch, nor relax from them in any instance whatever, unless imperious circumstances shd. render the measure indispensible.*
>
> —George Washington to
> Alexander Hamilton, 1794

134 What did Washington do after leaving the presidency?

The same things he did after resigning his Continental army commission: he returned to Mount Vernon to put his domestic affairs in order, and to await old age in tranquility. "Worn out in a manner by the toils of my past labour," Washington was sure that he would never again enter the public sphere.

> *I am now enjoying domestic ease under the shadow of my own Vine, & my own Fig tree; & in a small Villa, with the implements of Husbandry & Lambkins around me, I expect to glide gently down the stream of life, 'till I am entombed in the dreary mansions of my Fathers.*
>
> —George Washington to
> Adrienne Lafayette, 1784

135 Did Washington die of syphilis?

Absolutely no. Of all the myths about George Washington, perhaps none other is so grounded in ignorance. Washington died on 14 December 1799, at the age of sixty-seven. Hardly any other death in eighteenth-century America was better chronicled. Attending him were three doctors, family members, plantation workers, and slaves. At the time, Washington's personal secretary left two separate accounts of Washington's last illness and death; the doctors each left accounts as well; and later, Washington's adopted stepgrandson, George Washington Parke Custis gave his recollections of Washington's death. All were widely publicized.

> *The most outrageous lies that can be invented will find believers if a man only tells them with all his might.*
> —Mark Twain,
> San Francisco *Alta California*, 1867

Syphilis is a sexually transmitted disease caused by the *Treponema pallidum* spirochete (bacterium). After incubation the disease first produces minor symptoms, usually a single small painless sore, that heals without treatment. At the next stage a minor skin rash develops, sometimes accompanied by fatigue, loss of appetite, sore throat, fever, headache, muscle ache, weight loss, hair loss, and swollen lymph glands. These symptoms also eventually subside without treatment, signifying the onslaught of the disease's final stages. Sometimes latent for years, the latter stage of syphilis is more dangerous and can permanently damage the cardiovascular system. Symptoms include painful lesions on the skin, ligaments, joints, and bones as well as numbness, muscle weakness, paralysis, numbness, blindness, dementia, and mental illness. It sometimes causes brain aneurysm and death. Symptoms of the disease were widely recognized long before the eighteenth century.

No one who has ever espoused the myth that Washington died of syphilis has ever attempted to link any of the disease's symptoms to Washington's last illness, nor have they claimed that any of his symptoms mimicked those of syphilis. Rather, they just mindlessly repeat the canard.

136 What is the true story about Washington's last illness and death?

This is the truth of the matter: On 12 December 1799, as was his daily custom, Washington mounted his horse to ride about his Mount Vernon estate, which consisted of five plantations covering more than eight thousand acres. Although a few weeks shy of his sixty-eighth birthday, he was in excellent health, vigorous both in mind and in body. The ex-president stayed outside from about 10:00 A.M. to 3:00 P.M. The thermometer did not rise above thirty degrees Fahrenheit all day, the Northeast winds were strong, and until about 1:00 P.M. a drenching mixture of rain, snow, hail, and sleet was falling. Washington came in for dinner and spent the evening as usual, but the next morning he was prevented from riding out by a heavy snow that had fallen during the night. He complained of a sore throat but later in the day went outside to mark some trees that he thought needed to be cut down. That evening his voice was hoarse but he was cheerful and read aloud from his studies. When advised by his secretary, Tobias Lear, to take something for his throat, he replied, "you know I never take any thing for a cold. Let it go as it came."

Washington went to bed at his usual time but awoke between 2:00 and 3:00 A.M., agitated and breathing with difficulty. His wife Martha wanted to call a servant but he prevented her from doing so until it was time to rise. Once up, an overseer was sent for, that he might bleed him, a doctor was called for, and a "mixture of Molasses, Vinegar & butter was prepared to try its effects in his throat; but he could not swallow a drop." Washington already was beginning to die of slow suffocation. Bleeding brought on relief but not a cure, as did the doctor's preparations of a "gargle of Vinegar & sage tea" and a "blister of Cantharides on the throat." Another gargle of vinegar and hot water nearly suffocated him.

More bleedings, more doctors—but no relief. About 5:00 P.M. Washington told one of the doctors, James Craik, with whom he had been close friends since the French and Indian War, "Doctor, I die hard; but I am not afraid to go; I believed from my first attack that I should not survive it; my breath can not last long." From then on Washington was "uneasy & restless," and applications about 8:00 P.M. of "blisters and cataplasms of wheat bran to his legs and feet" produced no changes. Two of the three doctors left his room, "without a ray of hope." Washington died between 10:00 and 11:00 P.M. "During his whole illness he spoke but seldom," wrote Lear, "and with great difficulty; and in so low & broken a voice as at times hardly to be understood. His patience, fortitude, & resignation never forsook him for a moment."

137 So how did George Washington die?

Medical speculation has ranged from diphtheria to streptococcus to "fulminant cervical phlegmon" to acute epiglottitis to "profound hypotesion and shock" brought on by rapid bloodletting. Doctors Craik and Elisha Dick a few days after Washington's demise gave the cause of death in the Alexandria, Virginia, newspaper, as an "inflammatory affection of the upper part of the windpipe, called in technical language, cynanche trachealis." In laymen's terms an inflammation of the glottis, larynx, or upper part of the trachea. Antibiotics certainly would have revived him, had they been discovered; likewise, a tracheotomy might have saved him, and was even suggested by one of the attending physicians, but the procedure was so new that the doctors did not dare risk performing it. There is no consensus, but most medical authorities now agree that the bleeding was not sufficient to kill Washington, and it actually brought him some relief, as observed by those who were with him. The modern diagnosis of acute bacterial epiglottitis accounts for all of the symptoms, and agrees with the original assessment by the doctors who treated him. The infection caused Washington's epiglottis to swell, blocking his windpipe, and he suffocated.

138 What did Martha do after Washington's death?

While Washington lay dying his wife of fifty years sat at the foot of his bed in silent grief, foreshadowing the mood that would characterize the last two years of her life. When he expired her reaction was to say, "'Tis well. All is now over I shall soon follow him! I have no more trials to pass through!" She did not attend the funeral, which took place at the old family vault a few hundred yards from the Mount Vernon mansion.

After Washington's death Martha forsook the second-floor bedroom at Mount Vernon where she and her husband had so long slept together. She moved to a tiny room on the third floor where she spent much of the remaining two years of her life. Sometime before her death in 1802 she destroyed the correspondence between her and George, opting to keep private the lives they had shared.

139 Was Washington secretly baptized a Roman Catholic on his deathbed?

No, nor a Baptist, Presbyterian, or any other faith. In fact, during the two days of his fatal illness he did not even call for a minister of his own, Episcopal, faith even though there was ample time to do so. Likewise, the story that Washington demanded to be baptized by immersion during the Revolutionary War is a nineteenth-century myth. Washington was baptized by sprinkling as an infant into the Church of England, and in the 1760s he reaffirmed by oath his commitment to the Church's doctrine.

140 Why was Washington called the Father of His Country?

Because he more than any other single individual symbolized the American commitment to the republican experiment in self-government. Ancient republican governments often relied on a heroic protector of liberty—a wise, caring, and selfless figure who would appear on the public stage at critical moments—who would disinterestedly serve the people and then retire to private life. The phrase entered the public consciousness during the Revolutionary War, and by the time of Washington's death in 1799 was used in America and abroad.

> *All ranks and professions expressed their feelings, in loud acclamations, and with rapture hailed the arrival of the Father of his Country.*
> —Report of Washington's entrance into
> New York City to take the helm of
> the new national government, 1789

141 Why was Washington called first in war, first in peace, and first in the hearts of his countrymen?

Washington was called first in these things because he was. Before anyone else he went to war with the French, and long before others he anticipated war with the British. His compatriots recognized his primacy by making him commander in chief of the Continental army. After the war Washington's cohorts recognized his indispensable role in the Revolution by making him first at the Constitutional Convention, electing him its president. When the Constitution was ratified, he was elected first president of the United States, with unanimous consent. As president, Washington set all the precedents for the office. While serving as president he was the first to advocate neutrality when the French went to war with the British, and when it looked like the country would go to war with France he was again first, this time as

117

commander in chief of the army. Washington's public service did not go unrecognized by his contemporaries; he was America's first national hero.

> *First in war—first in peace—and first in the hearts of his countrymen, he was second to none in the humble and endearing scenes of private life; pious, just, humane, temperate and sincere; uniform, dignified and commanding, his example was as edifying to all around him, as were the effects of that example lasting.*
>
> —Henry ("Light-Horse") Lee, Jr.,
> Eulogy for George Washington, 1799

142 What is Washington's legacy?

Washington spent at least four years thinking about what he would leave as his legacy to the people of the United States, and to history. The result was a personal message that served as the self-styled "closing act" of his presidential administration—his Farewell Address. Both an exhortation and a warning to the American public, his "counsels of an old and affectionate friend" is a lasting testimony of what he had learned during a near half century of public service. The central theme of the Farewell Address is the importance of a strong American Union, based on the Constitution.

> *The Unity of Government which constitutes you one people is also now dear to you. It is justly so; for it is a main Pillar in the Edifice of your real independence, the support of your tranquillity at home; your peace abroad; of your safety; of your prosperity; of that very Liberty which you so highly prize. . . . it is of infinite moment, that you should properly estimate the immense value of your national Union to your collective & individual happiness; that you should cherish a cordial, habitual & immoveable attachment to it.*
>
> —George Washington's Farewell Address, 1796

143 What is Washington's legacy for today?

Washington's legacy remains for us what it was in the generations that immediately followed him. Certainly his indispensable roles as Continental army commander, president of the Constitutional Convention, and first United States president set an example—in fact a gold standard—for public officials to measure themselves by. His courage and leadership and commitment to the rule of law and the supremacy of civilian rule remain inspirational after more than two hundred years. Moreover, every American can emulate Washington's devotion to private virtue and to religious liberty.

> *I anticipate with pleasing expectation that retreat, in which I promise myself to realize, without alloy, the sweet enjoyment of partaking, in the midst of my fellow Citizens, the benign influence of good Laws under a free Government—the ever favourite object of my heart, and the happy reward, as I trust, of our mutual cares, labours and dangers.*
> —George Washington's Farewell Address, 1796

Chronology

1731/32

Born to Augustine and Mary (Ball) Washington at Popes Creek in Westmoreland County, Virginia, near the banks of the Potomac River.

Note: Washington's birth occurred in 1731 by the Old Style calendar (Julian), and 1732 by the New Style calendar (Gregorian). The New Style calendar, which added eleven days and began the New Year in January rather than March, was not adopted by Great Britain and the colonies until 1752, however.

1743

Death of Augustine Washington, Washington's father. Hunting Creek estate renamed Mount Vernon by Lawrence Washington, and construction of mansion house begun.

1745

Returns to live with his mother at Fredericksburg. Attends school.

1746

Considers entering British navy but abandons idea at his mother's request.

1747

Leaves school to live at Mount Vernon with his half brother Lawrence Washington.

1748

Takes surveying trip to Shenandoah Valley of Virginia with James Genn, surveyor for Prince William County, and George William Fairfax.

1749

Appointed public surveyor.

1751
> Sails for West Indies with ailing half brother Lawrence
> Washington.

1752
> Becomes residuary heir to Mount Vernon after the death of
> Lawrence Washington from tuberculosis.

1753
> Sent by Virginia governor Robert Dinwiddie to the Ohio
> Country to challenge the French claims to the Allegheny
> River Valley.
> Journal of the expedition is published.

1754
> Appointed lieutenant-colonel of a Virginia regiment. Dinwiddie's
> Proclamation concerning bounty lands for French and Indian
> War service.
> Defeats French and Indians at Great Meadows.
> Attacks Jumonville, and surrenders at Fort Necessity.
> Ill health.
> Sojourns at Mount Vernon.
> Resigns commission.

1755
> Serves as aide-de-camp to General Braddock on disastrous
> campaign against the French on the Monongahela River.
> Becomes commander in chief of the Virginia forces.

1756
> Commands Virginia provincial troops.
> Takes military mission to New York and Boston.

1758
> Suffers again from ill health.
> Courtship with Martha Dandridge Custis.
> Marches to the Ohio as part of General John Forbes's expedition
> to Fort Duquesne.
> Resigns commission and is elected to the Virginia House of
> Burgesses.

1759

Marries Martha Custis at White House, Virginia.
Takes seat in Virginia House of Burgesses.

1763

Dinwiddie's Proclamation concerning bounty lands for French and Indian War service.

1765

Serves as commissioner for settling the military accounts of the colony.

1769

Disapproves of Stamp Acts.

1770

Journey to the Ohio and Kanawha rivers.

1773

Stepdaughter Martha "Patsy" Custis dies.
Approves Committee of Correspondence.

1774

Attends meeting at the Raleigh tavern after prorogation by Governor Dunmore.
Appointed by Virginia Convention as a delegate to the first Continental   Congress.
Presides over Fairfax County meeting that drew up the Fairfax Resolves.

1775

Elected to second Continental Congress.
Chosen commander in chief of the Continental army.
Takes command of the army at Cambridge, Massachusetts.
Siege of Boston.

1776

Occupies Dorchester Heights and sees British evacuate Boston.
Leaves Boston for New York.
Battle of Long Island and Washington's retreat.
Affair at Kip's Bay and Battle of Harlem Heights, New York.
Battle of White Plains, New York.
Loss of Forts Lee and Washington and retreat through the Jerseys.

1776 (*cont.*)
   Battle of Trenton, New Jersey.
   Congress invests with dictatorial powers.
   Receives honorary LL.D. from Harvard College.

1777
   Battle of Princeton, New Jersey.
   Winter quarters at Morristown, New Jersey.
   Moves toward Philadelphia to meet British General William
      Howe.
   Battle of Brandywine, Pennsylvania.
   Battle of Germantown, Pennsylvania.
   Winters at Valley Forge, Pennsylvania.

1778
   Conway Cabal.
   British evacuate Philadelphia.
   Battle of Monmouth, New Jersey.
   Arrival of D'Estaing's fleet.
   Rhode Island campaign fails.
   In winter quarters at Middlebrook, New Jersey.

1779
   Captures Stony Point.
   Sullivan sent to Indian country.
   Winters at Morristown, New Jersey.

1780
   Rochambeau arrives at Newport.
   Gates defeated at Camden.
   Arnold's Conspiracy.
   In winter quarters at Tappen (Totowa), New York.

1781
   Pennsylvania troops mutiny.
   Meets Rochambeau at Wethersfield, Connecticut.
   With army before New York.
   Marches with the French for Virginia.
   Defeats Cornwallis at Yorktown, Virginia.

1782

> At Newburgh, New York.
> Urged to become king.
> Provisional treaty of peace.

1783

> Newburgh Conspiracy.
> Cessation of hostilities.
> Circular letter to states.
> Definitive treaty of peace signed.
> Takes leave of army.
> Last meeting with his officers.
> Resigns commission, and retires to Mount Vernon.

1784

> Engaged in canal projects to connect the Ohio with the Virginia
>   tidewater.
> Working for union.

1786

> Annapolis Convention.

1787

> Presides over Constitutional Convention.
> Signs new Constitution.

1788

> Efforts to secure adoption of Constitution by the states.

1789

> Declared president of the United States, and inaugurated on 30
>   April
> Makes a tour to northeastern states.
> Death of mother, Mary Ball Washington.

1790

> Federal City to be on the Potomac.
> Assumption of Revolutionary War debts.
> Cabinet differences.

1791

> Makes a tour of the South.
> Gen. Arthur St. Clair's defeat by Indians near Wabash River.

1792

Elected to second term as president.

1793

Proclamation of neutrality.
Recall of Genet.
Jefferson and Hamilton resign from cabinet.
Edmund Randolph secretary of state.

1794

Monroe sent to France.
Randolph resigns, and Timothy Pickering takes his place.
Jay's Treaty, forcing British to evacuate western forts as stipulated
  in Treaty of Paris.
Whiskey Insurrection in Pennsylvania.
Gen. Anthony Wayne defeats Indians at Fallen Timbers in the
  Northwest Territory (now Toledo, Ohio).

1795

Signs Treaty of San Lorenzo with Spain, opening Mississippi
  River to American navigation and setting southern boundary
  of the United States.
Treaty of Greenville, by which Indian nations cede lands of
  present-day Ohio, Indiana, and Michigan.
Jay's Treaty ratified.

1796

Pinckney minister to France.
Issues Farewell Address to the People of the United States.

1797

Retires from presidency and returns home to Mount Vernon.
X.Y.Z. mission to France.
Preparations for war with France.

1798

Alien and sedition laws.
Virginia and Kentucky resolutions.
Commander in chief of the Armies of the United States of
  America.

1799

Last illness, death, and burial at Mount Vernon.

Further Reading

Joel Achenbach. *The Grand Idea: George Washington's Potomac and the Race to the West.* 2004.

Richard Brookhiser. *Founding Father: Rediscovering George Washington.* 1996.

John Buchanan. *The Road to Valley Forge: How Washington Built the Army that Won the Revolution.* 2004.

William G. Clotworthy. *In the Footsteps of George Washington: A Guide to Places Commemorating Our First President.* 2002.

Marcus Cunliffe. *George Washington: Man and Monument.* 1958.

Robert F. Dalzell and Lee Baldwin Dalzell. *George Washington's Mount Vernon: At Home in Revolutionary America.* 1998.

David Hackett Fischer. *Washington's Crossing.* 2004.

Douglas Southall Freeman. *George Washington: A Biography.* 7 vols. 1948–57.

Frank E. Grizzard, Jr. *George! A Guide to All Things Washington.* 2005.

Peter R. Henriques. *Realistic Visionary: A Portrait of George Washington.* 2006.

Robert F. Jones. *George Washington: Ordinary Man, Extraordinary Leader.* 1979.

Gerald E. Kahler. *The Long Farewell: Americans Mourn the Death of George Washington.* 2008.

Edward G. Lengel. *General George Washington: A Military Life.* 2005.

Paul K. Longmore. *The Invention of George Washington.* 1988.

Glenn A. Phelps. *George Washington and American Constitutionalism.* 1994.

Tara Ross and Joseph C. Smith, Jr. *Under God: George Washington and the Question of Church and State.* 2008.

Barry Schwartz. *George Washington: The Making of an American Symbol.* 1987.

Richard Norton Smith. *Patriarch: George Washington and the New American Nation.* 1993.

Matthew Spalding and Patrick J. Garrity. *A Sacred Union of Citizens: George Washington's Farewell Address and the American Character.* 1996.

Mary V. Thompson. *In The Hands of A Good Providence: Religion in the Life of George Washington.* 2008.

Index

Note: Numbers in the index refer to the numbers of the questions and answers, not page numbers

CPSIA information can be obtained at www.ICGtesting.com
Printed in the USA
BVOW030440110413

317864BV00002B/88/P